I0424610

The Huge Book of Cool Facts

by
Jake Jacobs

Kindle Edition

* * * * *

Published by Jake Jacobs at Amazon Kindle

1.

The most ever uranium costed was $135 per pound in 2007. The current price is somewhere around $25 per pound.

Reference:(https://en.wikipedia.org/wiki/Uranium_bubble_of_2007)

2.

Jim Jone's son Stephan survived Jonestown because he used a basketball game as an excuse to not return.

Reference:(https://www.youtube.com/watch?v=VWqACvTknls)

3.

One of the earliest "bust a cap" references is from the Texas Ranger who killed Bonnie and Clyde in 1934. "I hate to bust the cap on a woman, especially when she was sitting down, however if it wouldn't have been her, it would have been us."

Reference: (https://en.wikipedia.org/wiki/Bonnie_and_Clyde#Deaths)

4.

Hugh Grant's second middle name is Mungo,

Reference: (https://en.wikipedia.org/wiki/Hugh_Grant)

5.

The cheese Parmigiano-Reggiano is a large target of organised crime in Italy. From 2013 to 2015, an organised crime gang stole 2039 wheels of it from warehouses in northern and central Italy.

Reference: (https://en.wikipedia.org/wiki/Parmigiano-Reggiano#History)

6.

Samuel L. Jackson's famous role in "Pulp Fiction" was written specifically for him, as Quentin Tarantino wanted to work with him after he auditioned for "Reservoir Dogs" but didn't get the part.

Reference: (https://www.youtube.com/watch?v=OyHxYRtKeM0&feature=youtu.be)

7.

Heath Shuler, former Tennessee Volunteers and NFL QB, used to be a U.S. Representative from North Carolina.

Reference: (https://en.wikipedia.org/wiki/Heath_Shuler)

8.

The largest number of graves of any cemetery for U.S. personnel killed during World War II is located in Manila, Philippines. It has 17,206 graves. 16,636 of which were U.S. personnel.

Reference: (https://en.wikipedia.org/wiki/Manila_American_Cemetery)

9.

"The Slaying of the Spaniards" is the only recorded mass murder in Iceland. In October 1615, 32 Basque whalers were killed by the locals in the region of the Westfjords after a series of conflicts, after their ships were driven on the rocks and crushed.

Reference: (https://en.wikipedia.org/wiki/Slaying_of_the_Spaniards)

10.

The Nazis in Auschwitz used to call the weak and exhausted captives "Muslims."

Reference: (https://en.wikipedia.org/wiki/Muselmann)

11.

In 1980, Glenn Seaborg turned several thousand atoms of bismuth into gold by removing protons and neutrons from the bismuth at the Lawrence Berkeley Laboratory.

Reference: (https://en.wikipedia.org/wiki/Glenn_T._Seaborg#Return_to_California)

12.

"Safety coffins" were patented in the wake of 19th-century cholera pandemics, since people were often buried in a hurry, to prevent further contamination, and would sometimes wake up six feet under.

Reference:(https://thestorytellershat.com/2018/09/07/how-to-survive-premature-burials-through-19th-century-cholera-pandemics/)

13.

The second most populous city in Bolivia has a base elevation of 13,620 feet.

Reference:(https://en.wikipedia.org/wiki/List_of_largest_Bolivian_cities_and_towns_by_populat ion)

14.

During World War II, when loanwords were out of fashion, the Japanese word for saxophone had 19 syllables.

Reference:(https://japantoday.com/category/features/why-there-were-19-syllables-in-the-japanese-word-for-saxophone-during-wwii)

15.

"New Coke", which replaced classic coke in 1985, was considered one of the least successful launches of all time. However, the severe backlash ended up as a huge win when "Classic Coke" was reintroduced a few months later.

Reference: (https://en.wikipedia.org/wiki/New_Coke)

16.

Larry David did the voice for George Steinbrenner in the show "Seinfeld."

Reference: (https://seinfeld.fandom.com/wiki/George_Steinbrenner)

17.

In the famous 1912 chess match Levitsky vs Marshall, legend has it that spectators were so impressed with Marshall's brilliant winning move that gold coins showered the board. Contesting Marshall's claim, his wife Caroline "disclaims even a shower of pennies."

Reference: (https://en.wikipedia.org/wiki/Levitsky_versus_Marshall)

18.

Work Addiction is where people feel compelled to work because of the high they receive from working.

Reference: (https://www.healthline.com/health/addiction/work)

19.

There are 1,933 fish species from 47 fish families that can only be found in a single lake.

Reference: (https://www.journals.uchicago.edu/doi/10.1086/691535)

20.

Juliane Koepcke survived when her plane broke apart two miles above the ground due to a lightning strike. Still strapped to her seat, she survived a 9,000 foot free fall and then walked 11 days through the Amazon to find help.

Reference: (https://www.bbc.com/news/magazine-17476615)

21.

The Magpie is a common and ferociously territorial bird that will divebomb and deliver painful pecks to the heads, necks, and faces of people that pass by their nests. This is just a part of life in Australia, necessitating countermeasures such as makeshift spikes worn on helmets.

Reference:(https://www.theguardian.com/environment/2017/jun/28/when-magpies-attack-the-swooping-dive-bombing-menace-and-how-to-avoid-them)

22.

Live human volunteers were used in crash tests to prove the effectiveness of seat belts.

Reference: (https://www.youtube.com/watch?v=GWy0hHHECdM&feature=youtu.be)

23.

The Danish East India Company established the first trading outpost in India at Tranquebar in 1620. During their heyday, combined with the Swedish East Asia Company, exported more tea to Europe than the British did, but lost importance and finally left India when they sold the last outpost to the British in 1868.

Reference: (https://en.wikipedia.org/wiki/Colonial_India)

24.

When constructing a pool in his backyard, a man found human remains and coffins from the 18th century.

Reference:(https://www.nola.com/business/2011/11/15_coffins_unearthed_when_prop.html)

25.

The origins of the necktie go back to the 17th century. Louis XIII hired Croatian mercenaries who wore a piece of cloth around their neck as part of their uniform. The French named it "la cravate", after the Croatian word for Croats, "Hrvati", and the French word, "Croates".

Reference: (https://en.wikipedia.org/wiki/Necktie#Origins)

26.

Virgil Abloh, artistic director of Louis Vuitton Men, interned at Fendi with rapper Kanye West.

Reference: (https://en.wikipedia.org/wiki/Virgil_Abloh)

27.

It is claimed that the Kim Jong family doesn't urinate or defecate.

Reference:(https://www.dailystar.co.uk/news/latest-news/520819/Kim-Jong-does-not-poo-pee-urinate-defecate-weird-facts-mother-boobs-breast-golf-books)

28.

Millennials are not people born after the 2000s as a lot of people seem to think. Actually, it ranges from people born from 1980 until 2000.

Reference: (https://www.goldmansachs.com/insights/archive/millennials/)

29.

The Newport Casino, home to the International Tennis Hall of Fame and the first U.S. Lawn Tennis Association championship, was established by James Bennet in 1880 after he was kicked out of the Newport Reading Room for betting a friend he wouldn't ride his horse into the prestigious social club.

Reference: (https://en.wikipedia.org/wiki/Newport_Casino)

30.

There are over 40 dangerous radioactive satellites in orbit around Earth. One, Kosmos 954, already crashed in Canada in 1978 spreading radiation over 600 kilometers, eventually leaking into the U.S.

Reference: (https://www.sciencedirect.com/science/article/abs/pii/0265964686900950)

31.

During the Gulf War, when faced with extensive trenches of Iraqi soldiers, American forces decided to simply use combat earthmovers and bury the enemy soldiers alive.

Reference: (https://en.wikipedia.org/wiki/Gulf_War#Bulldozer_assault)

32.

The Kyshtym disaster, the third worst radioactive disaster in history, was kept secret by the Soviet Union for 18 years and spewed radioactive fallout over 52,000 kilometers squared.

Reference: (https://en.wikipedia.org/wiki/Kyshtym_disaster)

33.

In 2012, Apple paid $21 million to the Swiss Railways to use their 1940 clock design in iOS 6.

Reference:(https://www.businessinsider.com/apple-paid-21-million-for-swiss-railways-clock-2012-11)

34.

Cow magnets are magnets farmers feed cows to prevent health problems from metal objects they often accidentally swallow.

Reference: (https://www.apexmagnets.com/news-how-tos/weird-magnet-facts-cow-magnets/)

35.

Matt Leblanc, before he was cast in "Friends," was told by a photographer to go to a dentist and file a tooth as it was longer. Matt couldn't afford $80 for the dentist as he only had $11 left to his name, so he bought 3 packs of emery boards and filed the tooth himself.

Reference:(https://www.today.com/popculture/actor-matt-leblanc-says-he-had-11-left-he-got-t147935)

36.

Research shows that your earphones are indeed spontaneously knotting themselves. A string of 0.5 meters to 1.5 meters has a 50 percent chance of knotting in a confined space, meaning earbuds with the "Y" shape chord have at least as much or a even higher chance depending on length and agitation.

Reference: (https://www.pnas.org/content/104/42/16432.full)

37.

The Himalayan Honey Bee makes hallucinogenic honey that tribes collect.

Reference:(https://www.mnn.com/earth-matters/wilderness-resources/stories/worlds-largest-honey-bee-makes-hallucinogenic-honey-you-have-be-crazy-harvest)

38.

Over one million Americans spoke Norwegian as their primary language from 1900 to World War I, and more than 3,000 Lutheran churches in the Upper Midwest used Norwegian as their sole language.

Reference: (https://en.wikipedia.org/wiki/Norwegian_Americans)

39.

When applied directly to the eye, the Bëchëte medicinal plant is reported by tribes to have the effect of giving the environment greater texture and dimension, making it easier to spot animals during hunting. The effects are reported to be long-term, lasting days or weeks, not just a few hours.

Reference:(https://en.wikipedia.org/wiki/Tabernaemontana_undulata)

40.

"Killing Season", or "July Effect" in in the U.S., is a period of increased medical complications due to graduate doctors beginning residency.

Reference: (https://en.wikipedia.org/wiki/July_effect)

41.

The Royal Bank of Scotland was the first British bank to put a picture in its bank notes.

Reference: (https://www.bbc.co.uk/news/uk-scotland-scotland-business-47401363)

42.

The Chinese government has a army division consisting of 10,000 pigeons.

Reference: (http://content.time.com/time/world/article/0,8599,2049569,00.html)

43.

Teen Vogue published controversial articles "Anal Sex: What You Need to Know" and "Sex Work is Real Work" targeted to its audience of teenage girls.

Reference: (https://en.wikipedia.org/wiki/Teen_Vogue)

44.

World War I was a fragment war. The range of casualties due to fragments, artillery and mortars, was as high as 70% to 95%. Steel fragments do not come at the soldier like rifle or machine gun bullets but at high velocity. Nearly all of them move at less than 1,000 feet per second.

Reference:(https://www.theatlantic.com/international/archive/2013/04/could-body-armor-have-saved-millions-in-world-war-i/275417/)

45.

Robin Williams was paid $75,000 for voicing Genie in "Aladdin."

Reference: (https://www.latimes.com/archives/la-xpm-1993-11-25-ca-60882-story.html)

46.

The Inauguration of President James Polk in 1845 was the first inaugural ceremony to be reported by telegraph and to be shown in a newspaper illustration.

Reference:(https://en.wikipedia.org/wiki/Inauguration_of_James_K._Polk)

47.

The political lifestyle magazine "George" once had the largest circulation of any political magazine in America, partly due to the celebrity status of its founder John F. Kennedy Jr. To boost sales, Kennedy posed in the nude in a 1997 issue.

Reference: (https://en.wikipedia.org/wiki/George_(magazine))

48.

Glen Bell of Taco Bell is pretty much responsible for del taco and taco tia.

Reference: (http://whendidithappen.com/wdih/restaurants/1950.htm)

49.

South Indian actor Ajay Kumar has made an entry into the Guinness World Records for being the shortest actor, 2 feet 6 inches, to play a character in a full-length film and, in 2013, he became the shortest director in the world to direct a full length movie.

Reference: (https://en.wikipedia.org/wiki/Guinness_Pakru)

50.

Eminem's mother created a rap CD called "Set The Record Straight" directed at her son in response to Eminem's many disparaging lyrics about her.

Reference: (https://www.youtube.com/watch?v=0FKyRVk-HPc&t=1m7s)

51.

Australian sheepdog named "Coil" won the prestigious 1898 Sydney Trials with a perfect score using only 3 legs after breaking one of his forelegs the previous night.

Reference: (https://paulineconolly.com/2018/a-kelpie-called-coil/)

52.

Green Light teams were U.S. Cold War teams that, in the event of invasion, would infiltrate Soviet lines with a nuclear bomb strapped to their back. They would arm the device and try to get away before it went off, but it was thought to be suicide.

Reference: (https://en.wikipedia.org/wiki/Green_Light_Teams)

53.

There is a snake with a protrusion that looks like a horn.

Reference: (https://en.wikipedia.org/wiki/Rhinoceros_ratsnake)

54.

After the death of Cliff Burton, Les Claypool was deemed "too good" to join Metallica.

Reference: (https://en.wikipedia.org/wiki/Les_Claypool#Early_years)

55.

Julie Andrews' first film role was the 1952 English dub of an obscure 1949 Italian animated film titled "La Rosa di Bagdad" or "The Singing Princess" in English.

Reference: (https://en.wikipedia.org/wiki/La_Rosa_di_Bagdad)

56.

X-Ray techs have to image dead people as part of their job duties.

Reference:(https://theradiologictechnologist.com/what-is-forensic-radiography-the-dark-side-of-radiography/)

57.

When Lance Armstrong was asked in an interview what he would do if he could go back in time and return to 1995, the year he started doping, he said that he would "probably do it again."

Reference:(https://www.theguardian.com/sport/2015/mar/09/lance-armstrong-cycling-doping-scandal)

58.

Lance Armstrong still holds the record for fastest Tour de France by average overall speed.

Reference:(https://en.wikipedia.org/wiki/Tour_de_France_records_and_statistics#Overall_speed)

59.

Florence Nightingale believed that women craved sympathy and were not as capable as men. She also openly criticised early women's rights activists for decrying an alleged lack of careers for women at the same time that lucrative medical positions went perpetually unfilled.

Reference:(https://www.cambridge.org/core/journals/journal-of-british-studies/article/florence-nightingale-and-js-mill-debate-womens-rights/DE0A5C1A3EA2CE34DCE1082932DCDB7D)

60.

"Sneaker male" cuttlefish pull a Mrs. Doubtfire to mate. When a female is guarded by a larger male whom they don't expect to beat in a fight, sneaker males will simultaneously present female coloration to the guarding male and male coloration to the female. It works more often than not.

Reference: (https://scholarblogs.emory.edu/evolutionshorts/tag/sneaker-males/)

61.

In 1998, NASA joined with the United States Postal Inspection Service to launch a sting operation called Operation Lunar Eclipse, which attempted to catch those trying to sell fake lunar rocks to unsuspecting buyers.

Reference: (https://en.wikipedia.org/wiki/Honduras_lunar_sample_displays)

62.

Former Massey Energy CEO Don Blankenship lost a campaign for U.S. Senate after serving a year in federal prison in connection to the Upper Big Branch mine explosion which claimed the lives of 29 miners.

Reference: (https://en.wikipedia.org/wiki/Don_Blankenship)

63.

The murder rate in the capital of Venezuela is so high that each year 0.1% of the population is murdered.

Reference: (https://en.wikipedia.org/wiki/List_of_cities_by_murder_rate)

64.

The Florida fairy shrimp was discovered in 1952 to be a unique species of fairy shrimp specific to a single pond in Gainesville, Florida. When researchers returned to that pond in 2011, they realized it had been filled in for development, thereby causing the species to go extinct.

Reference:(https://www.biologicaldiversity.org/news/press_releases/2011/florida-extinct-species-10-05-2011.html)

65.

Fleece is made from shredded up plastic water bottles.

Reference: (https://www.reference.com/beauty-fashion/fleece-fabric-made-9ee92aed35fc7374)

66.

By law, you can cancel any flight within 24 hours, free or charge. The flight must depart at least a week away, and you have to tell them it should be free to cancel.

Reference:(https://www.transportation.gov/sites/dot.gov/files/docs/Notice_24hour_hold_final20130530.pdf)

67.

The U-shaped toilet seats found in public restrooms were originally designed to give ladies plenty of room to wipe without having to stand up or touch the seat directly.

Reference: (https://home.howstuffworks.com/gap-open-front-u-shape-public-toilet-seat.htm)

68.

At the beginning of the Pearl Harbor attack, many people thought it was a drill. One sailor said, "This is the best goddam drill the Army Air Force has ever put on!"

Reference: (http://content.time.com/time/magazine/article/0,9171,156005,00.html)

69.

The Colt Walker revolver was the world's most powerful repeating handgun from 1847 until the .357 magnum cartridge was invented in 1934. It was designed to be able to kill an enemy's horse in one shot.

Reference: (https://en.wikipedia.org/wiki/Colt_Walker#Legacy)

70.

Harrison Ford and Sean Connery starred as father and son in "Indiana Jones and The Last Crusade" despite only having a 12-year age gap.

Reference: (http://www.bubblegun.com/features/20indy.html)

71.

Technically, 1024 bytes of data is supposed to be called a kibibyte, not a kilobyte, which is 1000 bytes.

Reference: (https://en.wikipedia.org/wiki/Kibibyte)

72.

In 1993, the experts of Manchester academy of fine arts liked a painting and included it in the exhibition. Later, they found out that its creator, Carly Johnson, was four years old.

Reference: (http://hoaxes.org/weblog/comments/rhythm_of_the_trees)

73.

There is a hidden 8 in the middle of the 8 of diamonds.

Reference:(https://indianexpress.com/article/trending/trending-globally/the-eight-hidden-in-the-8-of-diamonds-card-is-blowing-peoples-minds-5455563/)

74.

The global Brain Computer Interface, BCI, market was valued at US$0.696 billion in 2017 and is projected to reach US$1.840 billion in 2023.

Reference:(https://www.businesswire.com/news/home/20180122005870/en/1.84-Billion-Brain-Computer-Interface-Market--)

75.

More than half of the oxygen we breathe come from marine photosynthesizers like seaweed and phytoplankton.

Reference: (https://ocean.si.edu/ocean-life/plankton/every-breath-you-take-thank-ocean)

76.

The most valuable heist in Canadian history involved 3,000 tons of maple syrup worth $18.7 million.

Reference: (https://en.wikipedia.org/wiki/Great_Canadian_Maple_Syrup_Heist)

77.

Madame Leota, the face in the crystal ball on the "Haunted Mansion" ride, is named after Disney Imagineer Leota Toombs Thomas who provided her face for the character.

Reference: (https://disney.fandom.com/wiki/Madame_Leota)

78.

The Loyal Wives of Weinsberg were part of the surrender negotiation where all women could leave with whatever they could carry and the defenders, men, would be imprisoned. The women carried their belongings and their husbands on their shoulders. Saving them from being imprisoned.

Reference: (https://en.wikipedia.org/wiki/Siege_of_Weinsberg)

79.

Chad Stahelski, director of the "John Wick" movies, was Keanu Reeve's stunt double in the "Matrix" trilogy.

Reference: (https://en.wikipedia.org/wiki/Chad_Stahelski)

80.

Tug of War was contested in the Olympics until 1920 and it is still a World Games recognised sport.

Reference:(https://en.wikipedia.org/wiki/Tug_of_war)

81.

Bill Hader and Jason Sudeikis are both hosts on separate GTA IV radio shows. Chelsea Peretti is also featured as a voice on the radio.

Reference: (https://gta.fandom.com/wiki/Public_Liberty_Radio)

82.

The wood frog can survive being frozen and thawed multiple times, as long as at least 35% of their body water remains liquid.

Reference: (https://en.wikipedia.org/wiki/Wood_frog#Cold_tolerance)

83.

A California aquarium once apologized for calling an otter "thicc," "chonky," and an "absolute unit."

Reference:(https://www.complex.com/life/2018/12/california-aquarium-apologizes-calling-otter-thicc-chonky-unit)

84.

James Naismith, the creator of basketball, was the first and only losing record coach in University of Kansas history.

Reference: (https://en.wikipedia.org/wiki/James_Naismith)

85.

Although being a giant box office success, movie theater business was less enthused about the movie "A Quiet Place" because the ambiance of the movie was such that any type of loud eating was shamed leading to people not buying any food. Cinemas normally earn more from food than tickets.

Reference:(https://www.theguardian.com/film/2018/apr/12/how-a-quiet-place-became-a-cause-celebre-for-anti-popcorn-crusaders)

86.

There is a "Roadkill Cooking Festival" in Marlinton, West Virginia.

Reference: (https://www.bbc.com/news/world-us-canada-37501036)

87.

When preparing for his role in the HBO Season 1 series of "True Detective," Matthew McConaughey wrote a 450-page character analysis for the pessimistic, under-cover agent turned homicide detective, Rusty Cohle.

Reference:(https://www.rollingstone.com/movies/movie-news/-reveals-the-four-stages-of-true-detective-rustin-cohle-177382/)

88.

Nuclear Semiotics is the study of how to warn people 10,000 years from now about nuclear waste, when all known languages may have disappeared.

Reference: (https://en.wikipedia.org/wiki/Long-time_nuclear_waste_warning_messages)

89.

Female fig wasps pollinate female fig plants by burrowing inside them to reach the flowers and afterwards the fig releases an enzyme to breakdown the wasp and absorb the waspie nutrients.

Reference: (https://www.youtubc.com/watch?v=a6jJzOc9gaE)

90.

Grapefruit interacts poorly with many blood related medications by blocking the production of a certain enzyme in your body.

Reference:(https://www.fda.gov/consumers/consumer-updates/grapefruit-juice-and-some-drugs-dont-mix)

91.

Pringles has at least 162 different flavors. This includes mushroom, pecan pie, and white chocolate peppermint.

Reference: (https://www.snackhistory.com/pringles)

92.

David Bain is a man accused and convicted of murdering his mother, father, and three younger siblings when he was 22. He was acquitted after a second trial in 2009 after having spent 13 years in prison. The retrial jury took less than a day to render Bain not guilty on all five counts.

Reference: (https://en.wikipedia.org/wiki/Bain_family_murders)

93.

Portugal once had a military coup that went so peaceful that barely anyone was hurt.

Reference: (https://en.wikipedia.org/wiki/Carnation_Revolution)

94.

Horseback riding can improve posture alignment for subjects with forward head posture.

Reference: (https://www.e-sciencecentral.org/articles/SC000022208)

95.

Until the 10th century there was no set way of appointing the pope. Pope Fabian was made pope because a dove landed on his head at an opportune time.

Reference: (https://en.wikipedia.org/wiki/Pope_Fabian)

96.

Over a third of Americans have an STD.

Reference: (https://www.nytimes.com/2017/09/29/health/chlamydia-syphilis-gonorrhea.html)

97.

Bananas weren't eaten in the United States until after the Civil War.

Reference:(https://gourmetnutsanddriedfruit.com/a-history-of-bananas/)

98.

Rowing races in Oxford and Cambridge University are "bumps races" where the objective is to physically hit the boat in front without getting hit yourself.

Reference: (https://en.wikipedia.org/wiki/Bumps_race)

99.

The Sun is made up of ionised gas, which is the 4th state of matter, plasma. It's not only the Sun but even lightning, Northern lights, and the Earth's ionosphere; they all are made up of the 4th state of matter, plasma.

Reference: (https://www.nasa.gov/mission_pages/themis/auroras/sun_earth_connect.html)

100.

There are neglected diseases in the U.S. which are largely ignored, undetected, and untreated since they primarily affect people in poverty. Toxocariasis, for example, afflicts an estimated 2.8 million African Americans and can cause of childhood cognitive delays and even epilepsy.

Reference: (https://www.ncbi.nlm.nih.gov/pmc/articles/PMC4154650/)

101.

Shirley Henderson, the actress that played Moaning Myrtle in the "Harry Potter" films, is currently 53 years old and was 37 in Chamber of Secrets.

Reference: (https://en.wikipedia.org/wiki/Shirley_Henderson)

102.

During World War II, access to beauty products were in short supply, so the woman adopted the slogan "beauty is duty" and used more abundant ingredients such as beetroot, boot polish, chalk, and margarine.

Reference: (https://myhoustondaily.com/beauty/history-of-makeup/)

103.

Despite having little demand for whale products, Soviet whaling fleets illegally, and secretly, killed over 180,000 whales, driving several species to the brink of extinction.

Reference:(https://psmag.com/social-justice/the-senseless-environment-crime-of-the-20th-century-russia-whaling-67774)

104.

A church in Spain has been under construction for 137 years and isn't expected to be completed with decorations until 2032.

Reference: (https://en.wikipedia.org/wiki/Sagrada_Fam%C3%ADlia)

105.

Suzuki Hayabusa, the fastest bike ever when introduced, was named so after the peregrine falcon, which can dive at up to 300 kilometers per hour, which is close to the bikes top speed, and also because it preys on blackbirds, which is also the name of the then fastest bike the Honda CBR1100XX Super Blackbird.

Reference:(https://en.wikipedia.org/wiki/Suzuki_Hayabusa#First_generation_(1999%E2%80%932007))

106.

Anxiety and depression increase in teenage years to early adulthood, although plateauing in adulthood. Symptoms show a small decline until older adulthood, until symptoms again increase with age until death.

Reference: (https://psycnet.apa.org/record/2006-03906-021)

107.

Queen Victoria used her middle name for her regnal name. Her first name is Alexandria.

Reference: (https://www.britannica.com/biography/Victoria-queen-of-United-Kingdom)

108.

In 1897, SA Andrée attempted to win the race to the Arctic, North Pole with the help of a hydrogen balloon.

Reference:(https://www.ststworld.com/andrees-arctic-balloon-expedition-of-1897-a-peek-into-the-doomed-north-pole-flight/)

109.

It's illegal to die in Longyearbyen, Svalbard, Norway, because dead bodies weren't decomposing properly because of how far north it is. If someone is dying, every effort will be made to ship them to the mainland.

Reference:(https://www.news.com.au/lifestyle/real-life/wtf/the-arctic-town-of-longyearbyen-is-beautiful-but-it-holds-a-deadly-secret/news-story/66b72833155f7710d650e912b47d444e)

110.

The term "Weapons of Mass Destruction" was used as early as 1937, to describe German bombers used in the Spanish Civil War.

Reference:(https://www.britannica.com/topic/Defining-Weapons-of-Mass-Destruction-917325)

111.

In addition to non-standard half hour time zones, there are countries with 15/45 minute offsets from standard time.

Reference: (https://www.worldtimeserver.com/learn/unusual-time-zones/)

112.

The Church of St Mary and All Saints in Chesterfield is known as the "Crooked Spire", because it's spire has heavily twisted and distorted a seemingly impossible manner.

Reference:(https://en.wikipedia.org/wiki/Church_of_St_Mary_and_All_Saints,_Chesterfield#Crooked_spire)

113.

Marketing has promulgated the idea that coconut oil is a healthy food. In fact, studies have found that coconut oil consumption has health effects similar to those of other unhealthy fats, including butter, beef fat, and palm oil, and many health organizations advise against its consumption.

Reference: (https://en.wikipedia.org/wiki/Coconut_oil#Health_concerns)

114.

Cremating a single body requires enough fuel to fill two SUV fuel tanks.

Reference:(https://www.theatlantic.com/technology/archive/2014/10/how-to-be-eco-friendly-when-youre-dead/382120/)

115.

Deaf people with Tourette Syndrome swear in sign language.

Reference: (https://en.wikipedia.org/wiki/Coprolalia)

116.

A gang called the "Lo Lifes" were obsessed with the Ralph Lauren Polo brand and popularized it as streetwear. They raided high end stores, stealing hundreds of thousands of dollars in merchandise. Co founder "Thirstin Howl the 3rd" also did a song with Eminem.

Reference:(http://www.dazeddigital.com/fashion/article/37368/1/bury-me-with-the-lo-on-film-lo-lifes-gang-new-york-ralph-lauren-shoplifting-80s)

117.

Russell Crowe's character in "Gladiator" was based on parts of at least four different people in history.

Reference: (https://en.wikipedia.org/wiki/Narcissus_(wrestler))

118.

Former Toronto Maple Leafs owner Harold Ballard once asked the arena superintendent if he could make pickles in the tank that circulated the cold mixture under the ice.

Reference:(https://www.pensionplanpuppets.com/2009/9/7/1014184/book-excerpt-leafs-abomination)

119.

A nit is the brightness measured in candles per square meter.

Reference: (https://www.leyard.com/en/blog/2017/3/30/how-is-brightness-calculated/)

120.

Pigs live in social groups and can purposely deceive each other.

Reference: (https://www.cell.com/current-biology/comments/S0960-9822(10)00917-6)

121.

The title of Emperor of Austria also included the title of King of Jerusalem, even in the Austrian Empire's final years, despite the region not falling under Austria's domain. This was a result of the crusades many centuries earlier.

Reference: (https://en.wikipedia.org/wiki/Emperor_of_Austria)

122.

After the band Weezer covered the song "Africa" by Toto, Toto covered the song "Hash Pipe" by Weezer as a response.

Reference: (https://www.spin.com/2018/07/toto-weezer-hash-pipe-cover-watch/)

123.

Sinan Reis was a Jewish pirate who served the Ottoman Empire and fought against the Holy Roman Empire and Spain.

Reference: (https://en.wikipedia.org/wiki/Sinan_Reis)

124.

Gelatin is a yellowish, odorless, and nearly tasteless substance that is made by prolonged boiling of skin, cartilage, and bones from animals. It's made primarily from the stuff meat industries have left over, pork skins, horns, and cattle bones.

Reference: (https://www.popsugar.com/fitness/Gelatin-Made-Out-What-84889)

125.

Nylon got its name only after 400 other names were rejected. Among them: Klis, silk backwards, Nuron, "no run" backwards, and Duparooh, DuPont Pulls A Rabbit Out Of a Hat. In-house, it was known as 66, for the 6 carbon atoms in each of the two chemical compounds that make up the fiber.

Reference:(https://www.northjersey.com/story/entertainment/columnists/2017/02/15/game-changers-nylon-fiber-changed-america/97252932/)

126.

Devil's Bridge does not refer to a specific bridge. Rather, it is a term about medieval bridges that were thought to be beyond the capabilities of man.

Reference: (https://en.wikipedia.org/wiki/Devil%27s_Bridge)

127.

89% of people who own a programmable thermostat don't actually program it.

Reference: (https://www.goodcheapandfast.com/articles/best-smart-thermostats)

128.

Only 13% of Americans eat enough vegetables, while 71% eat excessive amounts of saturated fat.

Reference: (https://en.wikipedia.org/wiki/Western_pattern_diet#Elements)

129.

The famous Nickelodeon green slime was developed by accident. The first show to use slime, "You Can't Do That on Television", had a sketch planned where food would be dumped on a cast member. Filming was delayed, and the leftovers turned green, slimy, and moldy. They were still used.

Reference: (https://en.wikipedia.org/wiki/You_Can%27t_Do_That_on_Television#Slime)

130.

Stephen King also writes novels under the pen name Richard Bachman. The photo used of Bachman is actually of King's agent's insurance agent.

Reference: (https://en.wikipedia.org/wiki/Richard_Bachman)

131.

The largest loss of life from a maritime sinking was the MV Wilhelm Gustloff which sank in 1945 with as many as 9,400 passengers and crew lost.

Reference:(http://time.com/4198914/wilhelm-gustloff-salt-to-the-sea/)

132.

In the comics, Superman never served in the army in World War II. The reason was that if he did, he would have ended the war in mere moments, but that would diminish the role of real soldiers at the time. So, Clark Kent was made to fail the Draft due to his X-ray vision during eye test.

Reference: (https://www.cbr.com/comic-book-urban-legends-revealed-49/)

133.

A NATO exercise in 1983 caused the Soviet Union to make preparations for a real nuclear war.

Reference: (https://en.wikipedia.org/wiki/Able_Archer_83)

134.

Four corners national monument isn't in the right place.

Reference:(https://www.cntraveler.com/stories/2013-07-01/four-corners-monument-quadripoint-maphead-ken-jennings)

135.

John "Chickie" Donohue, a merchant marine, completed the "Greatest Beer Run Ever" in 1968 when he snuck into Vietnam at the height of the war to find his three closest friends and buy them a beer.

Reference: (https://www.youtube.com/watch?v=D4WAUmyKDq0&feature=youtu.be)

136.

The more antidepressants an individual had already tried, the less likely they were to benefit from a new antidepressant trial.

Reference:(https://en.wikipedia.org/wiki/Treatment-resistant_depression#Switching_antidepressants)

137.

There was a failed attempt at building a Colorado summer home for the President of the United States. Funding included a scheme to have school children donate their pennies. Today, all that remains is a bit of the foundation and a white marble cornerstone dated 1911.

Reference:(https://www.outtherecolorado.com/journey-to-colorados-summer-white-house-that-never-was/)

138.

A police officer who claimed he witnessed Tupac Shakur's last moments said Shakur refused to state who shot him. When the officer asked Tupac if he saw the person or people who shot him, Shakur responded by saying, "Fuck you" to the officer as his last words.

Reference:(https://www.billboard.com/articles/columns/the-juice/6099260/tupac-shakur-2pac-last-words-says-first-responder-cop-chris-carroll)

139.

There are African penguins and they're commonly known as "Jackass penguins."

Reference: (https://www.youtube.com/watch?v=LVF9F28SY4c)

140.

Transient Global Amnesia is where the person suddenly loses hours of memories and then goes back to normal as if nothing out of the ordinary has happened.

Reference: (https://en.wikipedia.org/wiki/Transient_global_amnesia)

141.

A fertility doctor used his own sperm to father 48 children.

Reference:(https://www.msn.com/en-ie/news/world/48-kids-discover-real-dad-is-mother-s-doctor-who-inseminated-women-with-own-sperm/ar-BBUXsEt)

142.

Margaret Thatcher was the last politician named in Pink Floyd's album "The Final Cut" to die. She died in April 2013.

Reference: (https://genius.com/Pink-floyd-the-fletcher-memorial-home-lyrics)

143.

Hamsters temporarily store food in their roomy cheek pouches, which extend to their hips. They can store up to 20% of their body weight and do not produce saliva to keep the food dry.

Reference: (http://jeb.biologists.org/content/210/17/ii)

144.

In many countries, including Australia, Invertebrates do not fall under animal protection laws and ethics, with the occasional exception of Cephalopods: Octopuses, Squids and Cuttlefish.

Reference:(http://theconversation.com/when-is-an-animal-not-an-animal-research-ethics-draws-the-line-21756)

145.

The phrase "sold down the river," signifying a serious betrayal, is derived from the 19th century practice of selling slaves for transport down the Mississippi and Ohio Rivers out of Kentucky. Kentucky was one of the so-called "slave-growing states," after importation of slaves ceased in 1808.

Reference:(https://www.npr.org/sections/codeswitch/2014/01/27/265421504/what-does-sold-down-the-river-really-mean-the-answer-isnt-pretty)

146.

Fred Astaire got into show business after his mother planned a then-popular "brother and sister act" in vaudeville with his sister Adele. Fred refused to learn to dance at first, but eventually learned by mimicking his sister's steps.

Reference:(https://en.wikipedia.org/wiki/Fred_Astaire#1899%E2%80%931917:_Early_life_and_career)

147.

After a two-year impasse with no new Pope, the Cardinals elected a hermit monk who sent them an angry letter, threatening them with divine judgement. He became Celestine V. He served for five months before implementing a law that allowed Popes to abdicate. He abdicated a week later.

Reference: (https://en.wikipedia.org/wiki/Pope_Celestine_V)

148.

The first time in history a British Naval Squadron fully surrendered was during the War of 1812 to American Commodore Oliver Hazard Perry in The Battle of Lake Erie.

Reference: (https://en.wikipedia.org/wiki/Battle_of_Lake_Erie)

149.

In 2009, a molecular biologist discovered a gene mutation that prevents fruit flies from getting drunk. She dubbed it "Happyhour". The same scientist had earlier identified mutations causing super-sensitivity and increased tolerance to alcohol, calling them "Cheapdate" and "Hangover", respectively.

Reference: (https://www.bionews.org.uk/page_91087)

150.

In Indiana, a cat attacked an intruder, protecting its owner and kept attacking him until police came and arrested the intruder.

Reference:(https://www.wideopenpets.com/binky-the-cat-attacks-intruder-with-nothing-but-his-teeth/)

151.

Despite solitary confinement being known for many detrimental psychological effects, many prison authorities consider it an administrative placement measure rather than a punishment.

Reference: (https://en.wikipedia.org/wiki/Solitary_confinement)

152.

Companies will intentionally alter the sounds of their products. For example, they will make a car engine sound louder as to make us think it is more powerful or make a vacuum cleaner louder to make us think it is sucking up more dirt and dust.

Reference: (https://en.wikipedia.org/wiki/Active_sound_design)

153.

Venus is so bright it can cast shadows.

Reference: (https://science.nasa.gov/science-news/science-at-nasa/2005/28nov_venusshadows)

154.

A bumblebee generates a positive charge by flapping its wings and transfers some to a flower it lands on, making other bumblebees easier to sense that pollen of the flower has recently been removed.

Reference:(https://www.npr.org/2013/02/22/172611866/honey-its-electric-bees-sense-charge-on-flowers)

155.

Never eat a polar bear's liver because it is toxic.

Reference:(https://www.adn.com/alaska-life/we-alaskans/2017/02/05/the-perils-of-eating-polar-bear/)

156.

Pont du Gard was built by the Romans in 1st century AD to carry water. It is over 50 kilometers long and the whole aqueduct descends in height by only 12.6 meters over its entire length. The aqueduct formerly carried an estimated 40,000 meters cubed of water a day to the fountains, baths and homes of Nîmes, France.

Reference: (https://en.wikipedia.org/wiki/Pont_du_Gard)

157.

The Aqua Appia was the first Roman aqueduct, built in 312 BC, with a daily volume of 2.6 million cubic feet of water. It was over 10 miles long and it dropped only 33 feet along it's way, which was a major engineering feat.

Reference: (https://en.wikipedia.org/wiki/Aqua_Appia)

158.

Only 4 countries have a Jewish population of 1% or higher; Israel (73.60%), Gibraltar (2.00%), USA (1.76%), and Canada (1.08%).

Reference: (https://en.wikipedia.org/wiki/Jewish_population_by_country#Table)

159.

The moon "wobbles". This phenomenon means that although the same side of the moon always faces the Earth, we on Earth can see 59% of the moon's surface over the course of its orbit.

Reference:(https://svs.gsfc.nasa.gov/10836)

160.

In 1991, a local businessman running for mayor in Austin held a press conference to reveal that he was a former mafia hitman from New Jersey who'd changed his name and relocated to Texas as part of the Witness Protection Program.

Reference: (https://www.deseretnews.com/article/155159/MAYORAL-CANDIDATE-ADMITS-HE-WAS-ONCE-A-HITMAN-FOR-MAFIA.html)

161.

Millennium Prize Problems are seven problems in mathematics. A correct solution to any of the problems gets awarded $1 million to the discoverer(s). To date, the only problem to have been solved is the Poincaré conjecture, solved by Grigori Perelman in 2003 who declined the prize money of $1 million.

Reference: (https://en.wikipedia.org/wiki/Millennium_Prize_Problems)

162.

Kids from the Ho Chunk nation receive $200,000 upon turning 18 and graduating. The money comes from profits from the casinos. Many of the recipients end up blowing the money fast with little to show for it.

Reference: (https://madison.com/wsj/news/local/hitting-the-jackpot-ho-chunk-mulling-changes-to-money/article_7e80b7e5-460e-5f6f-a7ce-bbb8d809d945.html)

163.

Mondo documentaries is an exploitive Italian film genre that began with the 1960s film "Mondo Cane". This genre generally depicts shocking topics about foreign nations or death with often falsified footage. The term "shockumentary" is often used to describe this genre.

Reference: (https://www.youtube.com/watch?v=G-SAri_0P8M)

164.

Magic The Gathering card artist Harold McNeil is a Nazi.

Reference: (https://www.coolstuffinc.com/a/mikelinnemann-040115-top-11-controversial-artists/)

165.

In folklore, "witch's milk" a term for breast milk produced by a newborn, was believed to be a source of nourishment for witches' familiars It was thought to be stolen from unwatched, sleeping infants.

Reference: (https://www.consultant360.com/articles/galactorrhea-newborn-witch-s-milk)

166.

Cubic zirconia has occurred in nature, the amounts were just too small use.

Reference: (https://www.jtv.com/library/article/gemstone-zircon-vs-cubic-zirconia)

167.

The first flavored vodka ever made was pepper.

Reference:(https://www.cwspirits.com/blog/absolut-peppar-the-first-flavored-vodka-in-the-world.html)

168.

If humans weren't able to sigh, the alveoli, air sacks on our lungs, wouldn't be able to inflate, and the lungs would fail, causing death. The only way to pop the alveoli open again is to take a deep breath.

Reference:(http://newsroom.ucla.edu/releases/ucla-and-stanford-researchers-pinpoint-origin-of-sighing-reflex-in-the-brain)

169.

With the help of Wayne Wheeler, the KKK was able to use Prohibition to promote a way to perpetrate state-sanctioned violence against people of color, Catholics and Jews.

Reference:(https://www.smithsonianmag.com/smart-news/why-racism-flourished-under-prohibition-180967406/)

170.

The Onagawa Nuclear Power Plant was much closer to the epicenter of the 2011 Earthquake than the Fukushima Power Plant, yet it sustained only minor damage and even housed tsunami evacuees. It's safety is credited to engineer Hirai Yanosuke who insisted it have a 14 meter tall sea wall.

Reference:(https://en.wikipedia.org/wiki/Onagawa_Nuclear_Power_Plant#2011_T%C5%8Dhoku_earthquake)

171.

Disney has its own government. The company petitioned the Florida State Legislature to let them govern its own land. In 1967, the statutes were signed and the Reedy Creek Improvement District was born. Disney have almost total autonomy within its border.

Reference: (https://en.wikipedia.org/wiki/Reedy_Creek_Improvement_District)

172.

The Atomic Demolitions Munitions, beginning in the mid 1960s, were Army Engineer Battalions of various divisions that were capable of deploying two types of ADM's, the medium or the special. It was a backpack nuclear device used to create an obstacle preventing enemy advancement..

Reference:(https://www.3ad.com/history/cold.war/nuclear.pages/nuke.vets.pages/adm.platoon.htm)

173.

The Grumman LLV, better known as the postal service vehicle, were produced between 1987 and 1994 making the newest Grumman at least 25 years old.

Reference: (https://postalmuseumblog.si.edu/2010/07/long-life-vehicle-llv.html)

174.

Golf balls were once smooth. Golfers eventually realized that old, beat up balls flew farther. Modern day golf balls now have dimples around them because they increase turbulence, which allow them to fly farther.

Reference: (https://entertainment.howstuffworks.com/sports/golf/basics/question37.htm)

175.

Zivi Nedivi was an Israeli fighter pilot who, in 1983, flew and landed his F-15 Eagle with one wing missing. The wing was sheared off after a mid air collision with an A-4 Skyhawk during dogfight training.

Reference:(https://migflug.com/jetflights/f-15-lands-with-one-wing/)

176.

ITER is an experimental nuclear fusion reactor still being built in France, the Project of which was initiated back in 1988. It is expected to be fully operational in 2035, to demonstrate the feasibility of fusion energy.

Reference: (https://en.wikipedia.org/wiki/ITER)

177.

Joe Son, the shoe guy from "Austin Powers," is serving life in prison for torture.

Reference:(https://www.thewrap.com/austin-powers-actor-linked-to-rape-is-subject-of-48-hours-investigation/)

178.

American film composer Bernard Herrmann managed to finish recording the soundtrack to the movie "Taxi Driver" just hours before his death on Christmas Eve in 1975. The film was later dedicated to his memory.

Reference: (https://slate.com/culture/2011/03/listening-to-taxi-driver.html)

179.

With a $7 billion almond industry in Central California, almond farmers pay up to $350 a beehive to keepers for pollination services. This creates a wave of beehive theft. More than 500 beehives went missing so far this year in this region.

Reference:(https://news.vice.com/en_us/article/kzdpey/stealing-beehives-is-now-a-thing-this-detective-is-on-the-case)

180.

The successful search for the Titanic was actually a cover story for the search for two downed U.S. Nuclear-armed submarines.

Reference: (https://en.wikipedia.org/wiki/USS_Thresher_(SSN-593))

181.

"Atomic Annie" is an artillery cannon that, in 1953, shot the only nuclear artillery test in the U.S. ever. Its yield was estimated at 15 kilotons, around the same level as Little Boy. It also had a backup version: "Sad Sack". Both are still around today.

Reference: (https://www.atlasobscura.com/articles/atomic-annie-the-nuclear-gun)

182.

Bob Hoskins was the first choice to play Wolverine in James Cameron's 1989 canceled "X-Men Movie."

Reference: (https://www.youtube.com/watch?v=4fjRHwY1qQU&feature=youtu.be)

183.

Bodyboarding originates from an ancient form of riding waves on one's belly. Indigenous Polynesians rode "alaia" boards either on their belly, knees, or feet. Captain Cook recorded seeing Hawaiian villagers riding such boards when he came to Hawaii in 1778.

Reference: (https://en.wikipedia.org/wiki/Bodyboarding)

184.

Disney's Space Mountain uses fans to blow air on you to create the illusion that you are going faster than you really are.

Reference:(https://www.getawaytoday.com/travel-blog/top-10-secrets-of-space-mountain-at-disneyland)

185.

In response to the "Y2K Problem", the Long Now Foundation was founded to "creatively foster responsibility" in the framework of the next 10,000 years; to address the "Year 10,000 Problem."

Reference: (https://en.wikipedia.org/wiki/Long_Now_Foundation)

186.

Foods containing peanut oil don't have to list peanuts in the allergen warning.

Reference: (https://snacksafely.com/2015/04/what-it-means-to-be-highly-refined/)

187.

Historically, in Lancashire, there was an alternative version of God Save the Queen that went "God save our gracious Queen! Long live our noble Duke!", referring to the Queen's role as Duke of Lancaster.

Reference: (https://en.wikipedia.org/wiki/Long_live_our_noble_Duke)

188.

Legendary director, actor, pilot John Huston once flew over a celebrity golf tournament and dropped 5,000 ping pong balls on it.

Reference: (http://www.movieactors.com/actors/johnhuston.htm)

189.

Healthy poop frequency can range from 3 times a day to 3 times a week.

Reference:(https://www.healthline.com/health/how-many-times-should-you-poop-a-day)

190.

The Great Moon Hoax was a series of six articles in The Sun, a New York newspaper in 1835, about the life and civilization on the moon discovered by a prominent astronomer at the time, Sir John Herschel. Apparently, the moon was inhabited bat-like winged humanoids who built temples.

Reference: (https://en.wikipedia.org/wiki/Great_Moon_Hoax)

191.

Yellow underarm stains commonly found on white t-shirts are caused by a chemical reaction between aluminum-based compounds, found in most antiperspirants, and sweat.

Reference:(https://health.howstuffworks.com/wellness/men/sweating-odor/antiperspirant-stain-clothes.htm)

192.

Canada has an act, The Good Samaritan Drug Overdose Act, that in the event that you need to call 911 for someone who's overdosed, you won't get arrested for possession of controlled substances charges, and breach of conditions regarding the drug charge.

Reference:(https://www.canada.ca/en/health-canada/services/substance-use/problematic-prescription-drug-use/opioids/about-good-samaritan-drug-overdose-act.html?utm_source=Youtube&utm_medium=Video&utm_campaign=EOACGSLCreative1&utm_term=GoodSamaritanLaw&utm_content=GSL)

193.

From the 1920s to the 1970s, retailers used X-ray machines to fit shoes.

Reference: (https://en.wikipedia.org/wiki/Shoe-fitting_fluoroscope)

194.

Abraham Lincoln had Confederate currency in his pockets when he was assassinated.

Reference: (https://www.c-span.org/video/?460076-1/lincoln-assassination-attending-doctors)

195.

There are, or once were, people in the porn industry whose role was to keep the male actor fully erect for his scene. This involved both physical and non physical acts.

Reference: (https://en.wikipedia.org/wiki/Fluffer)

196.

Germany's first crossroads-free motorway between Cologne and Bonn was opened to traffic in 1932 and downgraded to the status of "country road" by the Nazis, because they wanted to take the credit for building the first autobahn.

Reference:(https://www.dw.com/en/the-myth-of-hitlers-role-in-building-the-autobahn/a-16144981)

197.

Al-Aziz Uthman, Saladin's son and heir, attempted to demolish the great pyramids of Giza, but gave up when it proved too huge a task.

Reference: (https://en.wikipedia.org/wiki/Al-Aziz_Uthman)

198.

The Bechdel Test is a measure of the representation of women in fiction which asks whether a work features at least two women who talk to each other about something other than a man.

Reference: (https://en.wikipedia.org/wiki/Bechdel_test)

199.

Edmond Albius, as a 12 year old slave boy in 1841, invented the technique for pollinating vanilla orchids profitably. Without this technique, it's unlikely that vanilla would be nearly as well known as it is today.

Reference:(https://www.nationalgeographic.com/science/phenomena/2015/06/16/the-little-boy-who-shouldve-vanished-but-didnt/)

200.

The Monty Python "Doug and Dinsdale Piranha" sketch was based on real people: the Kray twins, London gangsters and murderers. They were among the last prisoners ever held in the Tower of London, in 1952.

Reference: (https://en.wikipedia.org/wiki/Kray_twins)

201.

There is a proposed ISO standard for sex toys.

Reference:(https://share.ansi.org/Shared%20Documents/News%20and%20Publications/Links%20Within%20Stories/ISO%20NWIP%20(Sex%20Toys).pdf)

202.

There is a giant pile of radioactive waste sitting at an abandoned military base in Utah.

Reference:(https://www.thedrive.com/the-war-zone/23704/heres-what-a-sinister-looking-giant-black-pyramid-is-doing-at-an-abandoned-military-base)

203.

Joan Ginther, a mathematician with a Stanford PhD in statistics, won the lottery 4 times already, accumulating over $20 million.

Reference: (https://en.wikipedia.org/wiki/Joan_R._Ginther)

204.

Chris Thomas Knight lived alone in the Maine wilderness for 27 years, surviving off stolen goods from local camps, having no fire for heat or cooking, and only speaking once to a passing hiker, he said "Hi."

Reference: (https://www.gq.com/story/the-last-true-hermit)

205.

On June 28, 1997, New York Yankees pitcher David Wells took the mound wearing an authentic 1934 Babe Ruth hat, which he had bought for $35,000. Manager Joe Torre made Wells take it off after the first inning because it didn't conform to uniform standards. It was later sold in 2012 for $537,278.

Reference: (https://en.wikipedia.org/wiki/David_Wells)

206.

The Who once wanted to make an album about their own history, called "Rock Is Dead—Long Live Rock" and accompanied by a television special.

Reference: (https://en.wikipedia.org/wiki/Rock_Is_Dead%E2%80%94Long_Live_Rock!)

207.

The creator of HBO's "Chernobyl" also wrote "Hangover II & III," "Scary Movie 3 & 4", and "Superhero Movie."

Reference: (https://en.wikipedia.org/wiki/Craig_Mazin)

208.

Bram Stoker, author of "Dracula," also wrote another book which was considered one of the worst horror novels of all time. "The Lair of the White Worm" has been described as "one of the most spectacularly incoherent novels ever to reach print", and H. P. Lovecraft called it "almost infantile".

Reference: (https://en.wikipedia.org/wiki/List_of_books_considered_the_worst#20th_century)

209.

Stripper poles spin, not the dancers.

Reference: (https://www.cosmopolitan.com/uk/love-sex/sex/a9999663/stripper-poles-spin/)

210.

There's a worm that earned the name "Eoperipatus totoro" because it resembles Catbus from "My Neighbor Totoro."

Reference: (https://en.wikipedia.org/wiki/Eoperipatus_totoro)

211.

Cheryl Ladd, from "Charlie's Angels", was the singing voice of Melody from the 60s TV Cartoon "Josie and the Pussycats".

Reference:(https://www.foxnews.com/entertainment/cheryl-ladd-charlies-angels-changed-everything)

212.

The "Eephus Pitch" is a very low-speed junk pitch used to catch a batter off-guard after a pitcher has been throwing higher velocity pitches, however, in today's MLB, it is a rarity.

Reference: (https://www.youtube.com/watch?v=IfyMbDnQY0g&feature=youtu.be)

213.

"Disumbrationism," an incredibly praised art movement launched in 1924, was actually a hoax by a man named Paul Jordan-Smith, who wasn't even a painter but a writer and a Latin scholar. He started this movement to spite art critics who criticized his wife's realistic paintings.

Reference: (https://en.wikipedia.org/wiki/Disumbrationism)

214.

Steven Gan and Premesh Chandran founded the only independent news source in Malaysia. Seeing a loophole in the country's Internet regulations they created Malaysialini, which was the first to criticise the government that had until then strict control of all print media.

Reference: (https://en.wikipedia.org/wiki/Steven_Gan)

215.

Wheelerism is a method of activism that focuses on only one issue and relies heavily on mass media to persuade politicians that there is widespread public support for an issue. It was perfected by a central figure behind Prohibition and master of single-issue pressure politics, Wayne Wheeler.

Reference:(https://www.smithsonianmag.com/history/wayne-b-wheeler-the-man-who-turned-off-the-taps-14783512/)

216.

The shrinking frog gets its name from its abnormal growth where it reaches a length of 25 centimeters as a tadpole before shrinking to a quarter of this size at adult age. This would be the equivalent of a teen growing to be 6 to 7 meters tall before becoming an average sized adult.

Reference: (https://en.wikipedia.org/wiki/Pseudis_paradoxa)

217.

The song "Move On" by David Bowie, played backwards, is "All the Young Dudes"—a song he wrote for Mott The Hoople.

Reference: (https://www.youtube.com/watch?v=xkJJC7Ssrhs&feature=youtu.be)

218.

Of the 14 "8000 meter" mountains, Annapma has the highest fatality rate of 34 deaths per 100 safe returns, including some of the most famous climbers in history.

Reference: (https://en.wikipedia.org/wiki/Annapurna_Massif#Annapurna_I)

219.

Echinoderms are the largest phylum without freshwater or terrestrial representatives.

Reference: (https://en.wikipedia.org/wiki/Echinoderm)

220.

We do not see only one side of the moon. Over time, due to what is known as lunar libration, we actually see 59% of the moon's surface.

Reference:(https://earthsky.org/astronomy-essentials/how-much-of-the-moon-can-we-see-from-earth-lunar-libration)

221.

Everyone that Madonna name-checks in the song "Vogue" is now dead.

Reference:(https://www.independent.co.uk/life-style/mortality-maths-like-the-realisation-that-the-last-of-those-name-checked-in-madonnas-vogue-died-last-9677382.html)

222.

If cats have too much catnip, they can "overdose" on it. It isn't lethal, but it does make then sick for a little bit.

Reference: (https://www.humanesociety.org/resources/crazy-catnip)

223.

The nursery rhyme "Mary had a Little Lamb" was written about a real girl named Mary Sawyer. She lived in Boston and her lamb followed her to school one day in 1816 when she was 10-years-old.

Reference: (http://www.newenglandhistoricalsociety.com/mary-little-lamb-yes-mary-little-lamb/)

224.

Melody Roads, invented in Japan, are highways that play songs. Grooves on the road surface cause a vibration and audible rumbling to be transmitted through the wheels and into the car in the form of a musical tune.

Reference: (http://goinjapanesque.com/04661/)

225.

There is a book called "Shadows from the Walls of Death", a book that's not only extremely rare, but also very lethal due to its arsenic content.

Reference: (https://www.atlasobscura.com/articles/shadows-from-the-walls-of-death-book)

226.

Lobsters are notorious cannibals, which is one of the reason it's hard to have lobster farms.

Reference:(https://www.npr.org/sections/thesalt/2012/12/03/166235228/caught-lobster-cannibals-captured-on-film-along-maine-coast)

227.

Coca-Cola originally was originally made from cocaine and alcohol.

Reference: (https://www.youtube.com/watch?v=1U4P9Fc-PbQ&feature=youtu.be)

228.

Duško Popov was one of inspirations for Ian Fleming's James Bond. He was a ladies man, party goer and double agent in World War II working for MI6, who informed the FBI about the impending Pearl Harbor Attack. Fleming witnessed a real-life bluff made by Popov and used it as basis for Casino Royale.

Reference: (https://en.wikipedia.org/wiki/Du%C5%A1ko_Popov)

229.

Pringles are not truly a potato chip but a "potato crisp" as they are made from a dough and fried. The can was developed by a engineer who wrote "Fantasy Fiction" and used a super computer to assure the shape and size of the can for minimum breakage on movement.

Reference: (https://www.snackhistory.com/pringles)

230.

When his girlfriend, Angie Everhart, was getting a minor breast enlargement, Sylvester Stallone entered the operating theater and instructed the surgeon to make them "big but perky", overriding Everhart's instructions.

Reference:(https://www.independent.co.uk/arts-entertainment/the-ugly-face-of-beauty-1071693.html)

231.

There are 20 bars of gold buried 40 meters deep in a World War I war grave, never recovered from the SS Laurentic.

Reference: (https://en.wikipedia.org/wiki/Lough_Swilly)

232.

Wile E. Coyote's middle name is Ethelbert.

Reference: (https://what-ever.fandom.com/wiki/Wile_Ethelbert_Coyote)

233.

Ptolemy's geocentric model works out perfectly mathematically, but is just plain wrong.

Reference: (http://abyss.uoregon.edu/~js/glossary/ptolemy.html)

234.

3 out of the 5 Founding Father Presidents; Adams, Jefferson and Monroe died on the 4th of July, Adams and Jefferson within hours of each other.

Reference:(https://constitutioncenter.org/blog/three-presidents-die-on-july-4th-just-a-coincidence)

235.

In Germany, a doctor diagnosed a case of cobalt poisoning because the symptoms matched a case shown in an episode of "Dr. House," and he wrote a book on how to apply Dr. House's diagnosis in real life.

Reference:(http://newsfeed.time.com/2014/02/07/mans-life-saved-because-his-doctor-watched-house/)

236.

Barra Airport is a Scottish airport so remote that it has no runway. Planes literally take off and land on the beach.

Reference: (https://en.wikipedia.org/wiki/Barra_Airport)

237.

There is a formula that draws itself called Tupper's Self Referential Formula.

Reference: (https://en.wikipedia.org/wiki/Tupper%27s_self-referential_formula)

238.

There is a language called "Esperanto", which was designed in an attempt to create a universal language. It has a completely regular grammar and allows the creation of a large quantity of words by combining lexical roots and about forty affixes.

Reference: (https://lernu.net/en/esperanto)

239.

If you take all the DNA in all your cells and put them together end to end it would be about twice the diameter of the Solar System.

Reference: (https://www.sciencefocus.com/the-human-body/how-long-is-your-dna/)

240.

Pudding Pops were selling great well into the 1990s but were discontinued because despite high sales, the company still couldn't turn a profit on them.

Reference: (https://culinarylore.com/food-history:what-happened-to-jello-pudding-pops/)

241.

The song "1985" by Bowling For Soup is actually a cover and was originally written and recorded in 2003 by the band SR-71 for their 2004 "Album Here We Go Again."

Reference: (http://www.cover-vs-original.com/song-94.html)

242.

A team involved in the visual effects on the movie "Bohemian Rhapsody" were not paid after Halo VFX, which oversaw them, went bankrupt.

Reference:(https://www.theguardian.com/film/2019/feb/27/bohemian-rhapsody-special-effects-halo-vfx-bectu-entertainment-union-cases-bankrupt-queen)

243.

Many NBA players have a pre-game ritual that involves Peanut Butter and Jelly sandwiches.

Reference:(http://www.espn.com/espn/feature/story/_/page/presents18931717/the-nba-secret-addiction)

244.

The most number of turns needed to solve a Rubik's cube in any scramble combination is never more than 20.

Reference: (https://www.cube20.org/)

245.

In 1861, Sarah Seelye, at age 17, enlisted in the Civil War disguised as a man to escape an unwanted marriage. Ironically, part of her duties involved penetrating Confederate lines "disguised" as a woman. She deserted the army after contacting malaria and resumed life as a female in 1863.

Reference: (https://tshaonline.org/handbook/online/articles/fse16)

246.

A crevice refers to a crack in rock while a crevasse is a crack in a glacier.

Reference: (http://mentalfloss.com/article/93624/what-difference-between-crevice-and-crevasse)

247.

All Europeans are related if you go back just 1,000 years.

Reference:(https://www.nbcnews.com/sciencemain/all-europeans-are-related-if-you-go-back-just-1-6C9826523)

248.

WhatsApp used to be a paid app that had a subscription cost of $0.99 per year.

Reference:(https://www.theguardian.com/technology/2016/jan/18/whatsapp-drops-subscription-fee-free)

249.

Using "ax" for "ask" isn't a new thing, and dates back at least to Chaucer.

Reference:(https://www.wnyc.org/story/why-chaucer-said-ax-instead-of-ask-and-why-some-still-do/)

250.

In 1992, a man named Stefan Mandel won a $27,036,142 jackpot, 6 second prizes, 132 third prizes, and 135 minor prizes in one lottery, by buying every single combination possible; over 5.5 million tickets. All 4.4. US states with lotteries have since changed their laws to prevent this.

Reference: (https://thehustle.co/the-man-who-won-the-lottery-14-times)

251.

There is a dating show in Great Britain on OTA TV called "Naked Attraction" in which contestants choose a potential date from among many options by seeing them naked. It features full-frontal nudity.

Reference: (https://www.channel4.com/programmes/naked-attraction/on-demand/63570-001)

252.

The same man created The Bigfoot and Stuffed Crust Pizza at Pizza Hut, McGriddles and Fruit 'N Yogurt Parfait at McDonald's and Smashfries, Veggie Frites, the burger and grilled chicken at Smashburger.

Reference:(https://firstwefeast.com/eat/2012/12/tom-ryan-smashburger-career-changing-innovations/7-the-burger-at-smashburger)

253.

"Arrack" is a type of alcoholic spirit from South Asia fermented from the sap of coconut flowers or sugarcane. Arrack predates all "New World" spirits and is the parent of rum.

Reference: (https://en.wikipedia.org/wiki/Arrack)

254.

The capital city of South Georgia Island, King Edward Point, has got only 18 residents.

Reference: (https://en.wikipedia.org/wiki/King_Edward_Point)

255.

Operation Babylift was the name given to the mass evacuation of children from South Vietnam at the end of the Vietnam War.

Reference:(https://en.wikipedia.org/wiki/Operation_Babylift)

256.

Marie Skłodowska Curie was the first and only woman that was awarded the Nobel Prize twice, married with Pierre Curie, had a daughter that was awarded too, jointly with his husband in 1935. This made the Curies the family with the most Nobel laureates to date.

Reference: (https://www.nobelprize.org/prizes/physics/1903/marie-curie/biographical/)

257.

Roughly 2% of the U.S. population, an estimated 620,000 men, died serving in the American Civil War. As a percentage of today's population the toll would have risen as high as 6 million. For every 3 soldiers killed in battle, 5 more died of disease.

Reference: (https://www.battlefields.org/learn/articles/civil-war-casualties)

258.

Luke Helder planted bombs in mailboxes across a number of Midwestern states. His goal was to create a "smiley face" pattern on a map, with each point being a location of a bombing.

Reference:(https://www.usatoday.com/story/news/nation/2013/05/15/mailbox-bomb-suspect/2164129/)

259.

A Taiwanese woman went to the hospital with a swollen eye, and doctors discovered 4 sweat bees living under her eyelids, drinking her tears. Her sight was saved, as were the lives of the bees.

Reference: (https://www.youtube.com/watch?v=JKb7sFnpP4o&feature=youtu.be)

260.

The Hole is a run-down New York City neighborhood that sits 30 feet below grade level and is disconnected from the sewer system.

Reference: (https://urbandemos.nyu.edu/2017/10/30/the-future-of-the-hole/)

261.

Henri de Saint-Simon had his valet wake him every morning with the words, "Remember, monsieur le comte, that you have great things to do." Later, he attempted suicide and shot himself six times in the head, but failed.

Reference: (https://en.wikipedia.org/wiki/Henri_de_Saint-Simon)

262.

There is an American, Spanish-language version of "Breaking Bad" called "Metástasis." It follows all five seasons of "Breaking Bad."

Reference: (https://en.wikipedia.org/wiki/Met%C3%A1stasis)

263.

Vincent Castiglia, an American painter, paints using human blood.

Reference:(https://www.bbc.com/news/av/entertainment-arts-19830950/blood-artist-every-painting-is-a-part-of-me)

264.

The Statue of Liberty was intended to be placed in the Suez Canal but was rejected by the Egyptians.

Reference:(https://blogs.voanews.com/all-about-america/2014/10/08/how-the-statue-of-liberty-almost-ended-up-in-egypt/)

265.

Table Tennis was invented by the British and "pingpong" is actually a trademarked name belonging to a British company.

Reference: (https://en.wikipedia.org/wiki/Table_tennis)

266.

There is still a Sheriff of Nottingham; the current one is called Patience Uloma Ifediora. Her role is welcome tourists and conference visitors to the city and to promote local tourism in the area.

Reference:(http://www.nottinghamcity.gov.uk/your-council/about-the-council/councillors-and-leadership/the-sheriff-of-nottingham/)

267.

The Earth would have to turn once every 84 minutes or 17 times faster than the current speed in order for humans to be thrown off the planet, when the centrifugal force would be bigger than the force of gravity that holds us "down".

Reference:(https://www.sciencefocus.com/space/how-fast-would-earth-need-to-spin-for-humans-to-be-thrown-into-space/)

268.

Mill Ends Park, the smallest park in the world is a 2 foot circle in Portland, Oregon.

Reference: (https://en.wikipedia.org/wiki/Mill_Ends_Park)

269.

At top speed, the wet weather tyres used on Formula 1 cars can disperse 85 liters of water per second.

Reference:(https://www.formula1.com/en/championship/inside-f1/understanding-f1-racing/Tyres.html)

270.

Rust doesn't cause tetanus. Tetanus, or lockjaw, is a bacterial infection caused by Clostridium tetani, an extremely hardy rod-shaped bacterium found in animal digestive tracts and soil worldwide. Humans can be exposed to Clostridium tetani in a variety of non-rusty ways, such as animal bites.

Reference: (https://www.mcgill.ca/oss/article/did-you-know/rust-doesnt-cause-tetanus)

271.

Yasuke, the first foreign-born samurai, was not actually a slave. In fact, he was a highly skilled warrior before he arrived in Japan. His training in Africa and India enabled him to become a samurai in a very short period of time.

Reference: (http://www.thelastdragontribute.com/why-yasuke-african-samurai-was-not-a-slave/)

272.

The language spoken in Wakanda is Xhosa, an official language of South Africa and Zimbabwe and John Kani, who played King T'Chaka, is a native speaker.

Reference:(https://comicbook.com/marvel/2018/04/07/avengers-infinity-war-wakandan-chant-tchalla/)

273.

The oldest movie with its main character's actor still living is from 1924. The actress was a child at the time and is now 100 years old.

Reference: (https://en.wikipedia.org/wiki/Diana_Serra_Cary)

274.

During pregnancy, the baby growing in its mother's womb needs plenty of calcium to develop its skeleton. If the mother doesn't get enough calcium, her baby will draw what it needs from the mother's bones. Women often lose 3 to 5 percent of their bone mass during breastfeeding, and recover after.

Reference: (https://www.bones.nih.gov/health-info/bone/bone-health/pregnancy)

275.

The lazy cops-donuts stereotype was the exact opposite of its origin: cops used to frequent donut shops in the past because they need to have work done and donut shops were the only ones that are open really early in the morning, to prepare for the breakfast rush.

Reference: (http://time.com/4800386/donuts-doughnuts-police-cops/)

276.

South Africans once wanted an Afrikaans translation of "Deutschland Über Alles" as their co-national anthem alongside "God save The King".

Reference: (https://en.wikipedia.org/wiki/Afrikaners_Landgenote)

277.

sea urchins got their name because they resemble hedgehogs, which used to be called "urchins." Sea urchins also used to be called "sea hedgehogs".

Reference:(https://en.wikipedia.org/wiki/Sea_urchin#Description)

278.

The Duryea Motor Wagon Company, established in 1895 in Springfield, Massachusetts, was the first American firm to build gasoline automobiles. In 1916, Duryea made an attempt to produce his own "car for the people" with a $250 car but only six were built due to lack of funding.

Reference: (https://en.wikipedia.org/wiki/Duryea_Motor_Wagon_Company)

279.

The Chinese invented a "south pointing chariot" for navigation in 1100 B.C.E.

Reference: (http://web.physics.ucsb.edu/~lecturedemonstrations/Composer/Pages/92.36.html)

280.

Deers would be considered legally blind by human standards.

Reference: (https://www.nytimes.com/2010/11/30/science/30qna.html)

281.

The Crown Heights Riot was a riot between African Americans and Orthodox Jews that occurred after a 7 year old boy was fatally struck by a car driven by an Orthodox Jew.

Reference: (https://en.wikipedia.org/wiki/Crown_Heights_riot)

282.

Palmerston is one of the most isolated island communities in the world. The tiny Pacific island is visited by a supply ship twice a year after a long, hazardous journey. What's more, most of its 62 inhabitants are descended from one man, an Englishman who settled there 150 years ago.

Reference: (https://www.bbc.com/news/magazine-25430383)

283.

Nepal was a monarchy until 2008, when they voted to leave monarchy as their system of government. They gave the king just 15 days to vacate the palace.

Reference: (https://en.wikipedia.org/wiki/Nepal)

284.

The idea for using countdowns before takeoff came from Fritz Lang's 1929 German silent film "Frau im Mond". Lang used the countdown to add suspense to the movie but the practice was later adopted by NASA to specify when various things happened pre-launch.

Reference: (https://history.nasa.gov/afj/ap15fj/01launch_to_earth_orbit.html)

285.

Sam Houston was removed as governor of Texas for refusing to take an oath of loyalty to the Confederate States of America.

Reference:(https://blog.chron.com/txpotomac/2010/03/today-in-texas-history-gov-sam-houston-ousted/)

286.

There was an Italian political movement which existed briefly after World War II that's goal was for Italy to be annexed into the United States.

Reference: (https://en.wikipedia.org/wiki/Italian_Unionist_Movement)

287.

With some restrictions, smoking is still allowed on airplanes.

Reference:(http://rgl.faa.gov/Regulatory_and_Guidance_Library/rgFAR.nsf/0/A8411424A90344 39862569050061F24E?OpenDocument&Highlight=sec.%2025)

288.

The number of stars on the EU flag is completely arbitrary and doesn't represent any number of states or anything at all. However, they are arranged in a circle to represent unity, solidarity, and harmony.

Reference: (https://europa.eu/european-union/about-eu/symbols/flag_en)

289.

Verne Troyer came from an Amish background.

Reference: (https://www.youtube.com/watch?v=M_EqXa2Mpuw&feature=youtu.be)

290.

A graffiti artist took Facebook stock in lieu of cash for work done at their first headquarters. When Facebook went public, his shares were worth $200 million.

Reference:(https://www.cnbc.com/2017/09/07/how-facebook-graffiti-artist-david-choe-earned-200-million.html)

291.

On average, raindrops fall at 20 miles per hour while drizzle drops fall at 4.5 miles per hour.

Reference: (https://hypertextbook.com/facts/2007/EvanKaplan.shtml)

292.

There is a Polish Movie "The Two Who Stole the Moon". It stars Lech Kaczyński, who served as President of Poland from 2005 to 2010 and his identical twin brother Jarosław Kaczyński the Prime Minister of Poland from 2006 to 2007.

Reference: (https://en.wikipedia.org/wiki/The_Two_Who_Stole_the_Moon)

293.

A resistor's color bands directly translate to the numeric value of its resistance.

Reference: (https://www.youtube.com/watch?v=IOb3-JZPY0Y&feature=youtu.be&t=335)

294.

Of the 72 movies that Arnold Schwarzenegger has appeared in, he has only said "I'll Be Back" in 12 of them for a measly 16.7% IBB rate.

Reference: (https://en.wikipedia.org/wiki/I%27ll_be_back)

295.

Hugh Laurie was on course to becoming an Olympic-tier rower up until a case of glandular fever forced him to abandon the sport.

Reference: (https://en.wikipedia.org/wiki/Hugh_Laurie#Early_life)

296.

The Iceland Deep Drilling Project is a geothermal system that supplies heat directly from molten magma. It can currently generate 36 MW of electrical power. Magma power is regarded as one of the more promising future renewable sources of energy.

Reference:(https://www.popularmechanics.com/science/energy/news/a23490/iceland-3-mile-hole-magma/)

297.

Troy McClure was named after Troy Donahue and Doug McClure. McClure's own daughters would call him Troy behind his back.

Reference: (https://en.wikipedia.org/wiki/Homer_vs._Lisa_and_the_8th_Commandment)

298.

The U.S. Supreme Court once ruled that Long Island was not legally an island.

Reference:(https://www.nytimes.com/2004/11/21/nyregion/long-island-at-its-best-whos-the-longest-of-them-all.html)

299.

The Mercedes 35 HP of 1901 is regarded as the first modern car. It dominated the Pau Grand Prix race from start to finish with a record average speed of 51.4 kilometers per hour.

Reference: (https://en.wikipedia.org/wiki/Mercedes_35_hp)

300.

In 2007, 2 years after being discontinued, the Pontiac Aztek sold only 69 units. Original GM forecasts in 2000 expected sales of 75,000 vehicles per year.

Reference: (https://en.wikipedia.org/wiki/Pontiac_Aztek#Yearly_American_sales)

301.

NASA lost communication with a spacecraft due to systems continuously rebooting because it can't process a date past August 11, 2013.

Reference:(https://en.wikipedia.org/wiki/Deep_Impact_(spacecraft)#Contact_lost_and_end_of_mission)

302.

The highest price ever paid for a coin was $10,016,876 in 2013 for a silver $1 coin from 1794, one of the first dollar coins minted in the U.S. following the Coinage Act of 1792.

Reference: (https://en.wikipedia.org/wiki/Flowing_Hair_dollar)

303.

Switzerland's Coat of Arms is explicitly protected under U.S. law.

Reference:(https://en.wikipedia.org/wiki/Wikipedia:Copyright_on_emblems#Usage_restrictions_on_national_emblems)

304.

According to Disney composer Alan Menken, the personality and musical style of Genie was inspired by Harlem Jazz and Fats Waller. He said, "The Genie of the Ring was described as being black, and having actually an earring in his ear and sort of looking like a hipster."

Reference:(https://www.billboard.com/articles/news/7825906/alan-menken-interview-songwriters-hall-of-fame)

305.

The myth that Jewish people have large hooked noses was debunked in 1911. Before the stereotype took hold, Jews were also depicted as having small noses as a way of falsely associating Jews with nose-cartilage-attacking syphilis.

Reference:(https://www.tabletmag.com/jewish-life-and-religion/278768/the-myth-of-the-jewish-nose)

306.

One of the greatest poets of the Middle Ages is known only as the Archpoet. Despite his fame, his name is unknown, and the only things known about him are what he mentioned in his poems. It's not even certain where his nickname Archpoet comes from.

Reference: (https://en.wikipedia.org/wiki/Archpoet)

307.

Queen Sālote Tupou III was Queen of the proud island nation of Tonga for 48 years. She captured the hearts of the British public at Queen Elizabeth II's coronation in 1953 when she rode with her carriage open in the pouring rain. This caused such a stir that she became a press favourite.

Reference: (https://en.wikipedia.org/wiki/S%C4%81lote_Tupou_III)

308.

Opossums kill 5,500 ticks every week.

Reference:(https://returntonow.net/2019/01/27/study-opossums-are-our-best-defense-against-lyme-disease-killing-5000-ticks-per-week-each/)

309.

Former guitarist for Blink 182, Tom DeLonge, quit the band to devote more time to his life-long passion; UFOs.

Reference: (https://www.spin.com/2016/06/tom-delonge-ufo-blink-182-national-security/)

310.

The Hippomobile, an automobile invented by Étienne Lenoir in 1863, made a test drive from Paris to Joinville-le-Pont, covering about eleven miles in less than three hours.

Reference: (https://en.wikipedia.org/wiki/Hippomobile)

311.

Melbourne, Australia gave some of its trees email addresses so residents could report problems. Instead, the trees received love letters.

Reference:(https://www.goodnewsnetwork.org/people-pen-love-notes-trees-given-e-mail-addresses/)

312.

The moulboard plough is a heavier plough that historians believe led to a huge increase in agricultural productivity throughout medieval Europe, leading to increase in population and growth of cities.

Reference:(http://www.medievalists.net/2013/06/the-heavy-plough-and-the-agricultural-revolution-in-medieval-europe/)

313.

In the 1800s, citizens that believed the Earth was hollow convinced United States President John Quincy Adams to approve an expedition to find the hole leading to the center of our Earth.

Reference:(https://www.smithsonianmag.com/smart-news/john-quincy-adams-said-yes-expedition-center-earth-180955203/)

314.

To figure out how bats and birds fly differently, researches watched bats fly through fog in wind tunnels.

Reference:(https://www.reuters.com/article/us-bats-flight/bats-and-birds-quite-different-fliers-idUSN1047841920070510)

315.

The Ancient Egyptians were able to test up to 70% accuracy that a woman was pregnant or not by having them pee in two different bags. One with wheat and the other barley.

Reference:(https://science.howstuffworks.com/life/biology-fields/ancient-egyptian-pregnancy-test-survived-millenia-because-it-worked.htm)

316.

Female "peacocks" are actually called "peahens", as the species is referred to as the Indian Peafowl.

Reference: (https://animals.mom.me/tell-female-peacocks-male-peacocks-8348.html)

317.

The Parotid gland is rather large, makes saliva, and can cause minor pain or tingling when drinking wine or tart foods.

Reference: (https://en.wikipedia.org/wiki/Parotid_gland)

318.

Ed Sheeran is the only artist to have a song streamed on Spotify more than 2,000,000,000 times.

Reference:(https://en.wikipedia.org/wiki/List_of_most-streamed_songs_on_Spotify#100_most_streamed_songs)

319.

The original version of "Ain't No Sunshine" by Bill Withers did not chart on the UK Singles Chart until 2009, 38 years after its release.

Reference: (https://factcompilation.com/interesting-facts-about-music-and-musicians/)

320.

The CIA planned a false flag attack to justify war with Cuba but was rejected by John F. Kennedy.

Reference: (https://nsarchive2.gwu.edu//news/20010430/index.html)

321.

Trees can have growths called a burl, in the U.S., or bur, in the U.K., and people actually harvest and sell these things for their intricate grains on the inside.

Reference: (https://treehut.co/blogs/news/what-is-burl-wood-its-weirder-than-you-think)

322.

Scientists in neurosurgery can monitor blood supply of the brain by stimulating the eardrum with audio. The amplitude and latency of the responses are recorded and compared to a baseline, allowing for rapid surgical responses that can prevent postoperative neurological deficits.

Reference: (https://en.wikipedia.org/wiki/Intraoperative_neurophysiological_monitoring)

323.

Balloon syndrome is a rare condition for hedgehogs in which gas is trapped under their skin as a result of injury or infection and causes the animal to inflate.

Reference: (https://en.wikipedia.org/wiki/Balloon_syndrome)

324.

The Kei Truck Garden Contest is an annual event sponsored by the Japan's Federation of Landscape Contractors. Landscaping specialists from around Japan compete to turn their tiny truck's bed into mini-size gardens.

Reference: (http://www.zoenren-osaka.jp/contest_nagai_h28.html)

325.

Eddie Slovick is the only American soldier executed for desertion since the Civil War, a sentence personally approved by Eisenhower.

Reference: (https://en.wikipedia.org/wiki/Eddie_Slovik)

326.

The first roller coaster debuted in Paris over 200 years ago. Passengers climbed a set of stairs to ride a bench down the 600-foot track at 40 miles per hour..

Reference:(https://www.npr.org/2017/04/13/523804466/200-years-ago-the-words-first-rollercoaster-debuted-in-paris)

327.

The "Qattara Depression Project" was a plan to partially flood parts of the Sahara, using 213 1.5 megatons nukes to "dig" the canal.

Reference: (https://en.wikipedia.org/wiki/Qattara_Depression_Project#cite_note-12)

328.

Researchers gave puffins sunglasses. They were investigating the bioluminescence of puffin beaks with UV light.

Reference:(https://news.nationalgeographic.com/2018/04/sharks-puffins-animals-biofluorescence-oceans/)

329.

There is a permanent colony of wallabies inhabiting an island in Loch Lomond in Scotland after being released there in the 1940s by an eccentric millionaire.

Reference: (https://www.atlasobscura.com/places/wallabies-of-inchconnachan)

330.

Alexandre Dumas worked with a uncredited collaborator who was responsible for much of The Three Musketeers books, The Count of Monte Cristo, and other novels. Auguste Maquet did all the research, created the plot and characters, wrote the first draft, and then Dumas then rewrote the dialogue.

Reference:(https://www.telegraph.co.uk/news/worldnews/europe/france/7198679/Alexandre-Dumas-novels-penned-by-fourth-musketeer-ghost-writer.html)

331.

The term "soccer" is actually British in origin.

Reference: (http://time.com/5335799/soccer-word-origin-england/)

332.

Drake's 2018 hit "Nice for What" sampled Lauryn Hill's "Ex-Factor," which sampled Wu-Tang's "Can It All Be So Simple," which sampled Gladys Knight's cover of Streisand's "The Way We Were." So the writer of "The Way We Were" is also credited on "Nice for What" but no part of his writing is in it.

Reference:(https://www.billboard.com/articles/columns/hip-hop/8378323/drake-nice-for-what-sampling-history-lauryn-hill)

333.

The HAL 9000, the iconic sentient machine with a male voice from Kubrick's "2001: A Space Odyssey" was originally slated to be named Athena and have a female voice.

Reference:(https://www.smithsonianmag.com/smart-news/2001-a-space-odysseys-hal-9000-was-originally-a-female-7623079/)

334.

The Citroen DS had its best sales year 15 years after having been introduced, in 1970.

Reference: (https://en.wikipedia.org/wiki/Citro%C3%ABn_DS#Replacing_the_DS)

335.

Dr. Leonard Baily, in 1984, transplanted a baboon heart into a dying infant known as Baby Fae. Baby Fae lived for another three weeks after the procedure.

Reference: (http://time.com/4086900/baby-fae-history/)

336.

With the exception of college or military service, 37 percent of Americans have never lived outside their hometown, and 57 percent of Americans have never lived outside their home state.

Reference:(https://www.nytimes.com/interactive/2015/12/24/upshot/24up-family.html)

337.

Bollywood has been huge in Russia since the 1950's.

Reference:(https://www.calvertjournal.com/articles/show/4569/bollywood-affair-indian-cinema-USSR-raj-kapoor-nargis)

338.

Dueling scars were seen as a badge of honor among upper class Germans through the mid-19th and 20th century. It was seen as ideal and a way of showing courage to be able to stand and take the blow.

Reference:(https://portraitofwar.com/2017/12/26/wwi-german-facial-dueling-scars-mensur-scars-and-wwi-portraits/amp/)

339.

In former Soviet territories there are hundreds of small, abandoned nuclear generators in total disrepair.

Reference:(https://bellona.org/news/nuclear-issues/radioactive-waste-and-spent-nuclear-fuel/2005-04-radioisotope-thermoelectric-generators-2)

340.

Sophie Turner adopted the dog named Lunni that played her character Sansa Stark's direwolf, Lady, after filming of Season 1 completed.

Reference: (http://nisociety.com/about-the-breed/game-of-thrones/)

341.

Stinky-finger Syndrome is a term used in Psychol Medicine for stimulation of the prostate gland and relief of constipation.

Reference: (https://www.ncbi.nlm.nih.gov/pmc/articles/PMC5688896/)

342.

Some of the very first air-to-ground radio transmissions were from the airship "America", and made about the ship's cat, Kiddo, in 1910. Airship engineer Melvin Vaniman said, "Come and get this goddamn cat!"

Reference: (https://en.wikipedia.org/wiki/America_%28airship%29)

343.

The song "Holding Back the Years" was based on the lead singer being abandoned by his mother when he was three years old.

Reference: (https://en.wikipedia.org/wiki/Holding_Back_the_Years)

344.

The Parliament building in Bucharest is so massive that even though it already contains both lower and upper houses of parliament, three museums, and an international conference centre, 70% of the building is still empty. The heating and electrical bill alone amounts to $6 million a year.

Reference: (https://en.wikipedia.org/wiki/Palace_of_the_Parliament)

345.

The first commercially successful internal combustion engine, invented in 1859, was decades past the end of the first industrial revolution, which was between 1820 and 1840.

Reference: (https://en.wikipedia.org/wiki/Internal_combustion_engine)

346.

In 1891, Max Wolf pioneered the use of astrophotography to detect asteroids, and used it to discover 248 of them himself. Yet though it was known that there were many more, most astronomers did not bother with them, calling them "vermin of the skies".

Reference: (https://en.wikipedia.org/wiki/Asteroid#Historical_methods)

347.

Tony Burrows was the lead vocalist for five one-hit wonders: "Let's Go to San Francisco" by The Flower Pot Men, "Love Grows Where My Rosemary Goes" by Edison Lighthouse, "My Baby Loves Lovin'" by White Plains, "United We Stand" by The Brotherhood of Man, and "Beach Baby" by The First Class.

Reference: (https://en.wikipedia.org/wiki/Tony_Burrows)

348.

Germany has an enormous underground archive to save the nation's cultural heritage from natural or manmade disaster.

Reference:(https://en.wikipedia.org/wiki/Construction_of_the_World_Trade_Center#Design_elements)

349.

Mawsynram, located in the Meghalaya State in India, is the wettest place in the world, with an annual rainfall of 36 feet.

Reference: (https://www.worldatlas.com/articles/the-ten-wettest-places-in-the-world.html)

350.

The tomato is a berry. Its English name derives from the Aztec word for "fat or swelling fruit," and its Latin name literally means "wolf peach."

Reference: (https://en.wikipedia.org/wiki/Tomato)

351.

For every bird killed by a windmill, around 1,700 are killed by cars.

Reference: (http://cleantechnica.com/2018/02/21/wind-power-results-deaths-overall/)

352.

Arnold Schwarzenegger's salary for "T2: Judgement Day" was $15 million and the total amount of words spoken by him in the entire film is 700. This attributes to $21,429 per word and the line "Hasta la vista, baby" amounts to $85,716.

Reference: (https://ew.com/article/1991/07/19/arnold-schwarzeneggers-words/)

353.

Some people have learned how to fish using tamed birds instead of using hooks or nets.

Reference: (https://www.youtube.com/watch?v=cS9wzAjbJ24&feature=youtu.be)

354.

Reparations were given to some 40,000 former African American slaves who were settled on 400,000 acres. However, President Andrew Johnson returned the land to the previous owners when Lincoln was assassinated and Johnson became president.

Reference:(https://en.wikipedia.org/wiki/Reparations_for_slavery_debate_in_the_United_States)

355.

Chinese youth used to listen to a lot of music CDs from the U.S. with holes punched through the corner. The so-called "dakou" CDs were surplus albums destined to be disposed, but ended up being sold in China instead. You could listen to most of each album, but some songs would be missing.

Reference: (http://www.dongting08.net/2008/06/deal-with-dakou.html)

356.

Schools can get 40% or 50% cut of sales from Lifetouch portrait sales, using signing bonuses and commission rates as incentives to win business from local school districts.

Reference:(https://www.nbcwashington.com/investigations/Money-Schools-Earn-From-Student-Portraits-Varies-Widely-369744951.html)

357.

During Medieval Europe, the use of pointy shoes started as a fad to signify status, but as the size of the toe-tips continuously increased, the English crown felt the need to intervene, because of "lascivious connotations".

Reference:(https://www.researchgate.net/publication/229797066_Masculinities_and_the_Medieval_English_Sumptuary_Laws)

358.

Elisa Lam was a Canadian student at the University of British Columbia who disappeared while staying at the Cecil Hotel in Downtown Los Angeles. Only later to be found in the water tank when guests complained of problems with the water supply.

Reference: (https://en.wikipedia.org/wiki/Death_of_Elisa_Lam)

359.

Prior to 1996, there was no requirement to present an ID to board a plane. The policy was put into place to show the government was "doing something" about the crash of TWA Flight 800.

Reference: (https://viewfromthewing.boardingarea.com/2015/12/14/42388/)

360.

U.S. President Benjamin Harrison had electric lights installed in the White House, but would sleep with the lights on because he was too afraid to touch the switches.

Reference:(https://en.wikipedia.org/wiki/Benjamin_Harrison#Technology_and_naval_modernization)

361.

Pico de gallo translates to Rooster's Beak.

Reference: (https://en.wikipedia.org/wiki/Pico_de_gallo)

362.

Due to intense metabolic demands of flight which in turn cause constant high levels of inflammation, bats have evolved ways to dampen their immune response towards the inflammation and this explains their ability to carry and transmit some of the world's deadliest zoonotic viruses.

Reference:(https://www.the-scientist.com/notebook/why-bats-make-such-good-viral-hosts-64251)

363.

There was a Mortal Kombat: "Live Tour", similar to a play that toured between 1995 and 1996.

Reference: (https://en.wikipedia.org/wiki/Mortal_Kombat:_Live_Tour)

364.

Muhammad Ali's original name was Cassius Marcellus Clay, Jr.

Reference: (https://www.britannica.com/biography/Muhammad-Ali-boxer)

365.

After the death of Princess Diana, radio station XFM banned certain songs that might upset people. Banned songs included "Drive" by The Cars, "Airbag" by Radiohead and anything by the Crash Test Dummies.

Reference: (https://www.stephenmerchant.com/about-me)

366.

Stormtroopers originally had lightsabers.

Reference: (https://screenrant.com/star-wars-stormtroopers-trivia-facts-rogue-one/)

367.

There is a species of tigerfish in the Congo River which eats crocodiles.

Reference:(https://www.dailytelegraph.com.au/caught-the-fish-that-eats-crocs/news-story/e4845f7a89f1f9546e1136a143467752?sv=d1ae594306bfabae6d01389d7a4d5997)

368.

Banknotes were invented by Chinese in the 6th century for replacing coins as burial money. They started using it as currency in 812. The oldest conserved banknote is called "Kuan", made of mulberry tree bark, and dates from 1375.

Reference: (https://www.nbbmuseum.be/en/2007/09/chinese-invention.htm)

369.
The Curiosity Rover uses a radiation hardened version of the PowerPC CPU that costs $200,000 each.

Reference: (https://en.wikipedia.org/wiki/RAD750)

370.
Bear Grylls and Drew Brees killed a crocodile by jamming a knife between its head and body. As Brees held the knife, Bear used a rock to smash it in. After, Brees asked Bear, "Do you know how much my hand is insured for?"

Reference: (https://www.youtube.com/watch?v=mR2VifNd-_E&feature=youtu.be&t=446)

371.
Blocking airflow to the eye can increase your chances of corneal ulcers. Besides possible creation of a bacteria haven, oxygen restriction is a major reason why you are recommended to remove your contacts and let your eyes "breathe" often.

Reference: (https://healthool.com/corneal-ulcer/)

372.
Soviet nuclear weapons remained in Cuba after the Cuban Missile Crisis.

Reference: (https://www.bbc.co.uk/news/magazine-19930260)

373.
Bacteria is used in the production of self healing and super strong concrete.

Reference: (https://www.youtube.com/watch?v=0HjgoyoVP7A&feature=youtu.be)

374.
Denim originally meant cotton woven in the French city of Nimes.

Reference: (https://en.wikipedia.org/wiki/Denim)

375.

The original Arthur book focused on Arthur's struggle to accept his lengthy nose, yet the Arthur we all know doesn't have that classic aardvark nose any longer.

Reference: (https://en.wikipedia.org/wiki/Arthur's_Nose)

376.

Aristotle believed that there were only three colors present in the rainbow.

Reference:(https://www.cambridge.org/core/journals/classical-quarterly/article/defence-of-aristotle-meteorologica-3-375a6ff/608C33054450B0049788FC2E8F2C42A2)

377.

In the 17th to 18th century, around 10% of the Norwegian population migrated to the Netherlands.

Reference: (https://en.wikipedia.org/wiki/Norwegians#Netherlands)

378.

The Kingdom of Bhutan only has one international airport, located at 7,332 feet of elevation in a deep valley surrounded by 18,000 foot mountains and only a select number of pilots are certified to land there, due to it being one of the most challenging airports in the world.

Reference: (https://en.wikipedia.org/wiki/Paro_Airport)

379.

Killing a president was not a federal offense during the time of Kennedy's assassination. Because of this, the medical examiner argued that the autopsy had to be performed before the body is taken from Dallas. Johnson ordered the body to be released, but the medical examiner refused.

Reference: (https://www.businessinsider.com/kennedy-assassination-timeline-2013-11#2-pm-16)

380.

The Burke and Wills expedition of 1860 is Australia's own Lewis and Clarke. Burke, Wills and 17 others set off to cross Australia South-North, from Melbourne to the Gulf of Carpentaria, a 3250 kilometer journey one way. Both men died. Only one, an Irish soldier named John King completed the journey back.

Reference: (https://en.wikipedia.org/wiki/Burke_and_Wills_expedition)

381.

The Russian women's volleyball coach, Sergei Ovchinnikov, committed suicide after the team failed to beat Brazil in the 2012 Summer Olympics Quarterfinals.

Reference: (https://en.wikipedia.org/wiki/Sergei_Ovchinnikov_(volleyball))

382.

Pythagoras, known for his famous mathematical theorem, is also the father of vegetarianism.

Reference: (https://www.history.com/news/beans-and-greens-the-history-of-vegetarianism)

383.

Adolphe Sax, the inventor of the saxophone, survived a three story fall, a gunpowder explosion, drinking a bowl of sulfuric water, a near-poisoning due to furniture varnish, and falling into a speeding river, all before the age of nine. His neighbors called him "Little Sax, the ghost".

Reference: (https://en.wikipedia.org/wiki/Adolphe_Sax)

384.

It's a myth that sex workers don't kiss clients. Clients just have to pay for the intimate privilege of The Girlfriend Experience, which includes open mouth kissing including tongue. it emphasizes "authenticity" and "connection".

Reference:(https://www.bodyandsoul.com.au/sex-relationships/sex/owo-dfk-ro-the-slang-sex-workers-use-explained/news-story/eb30efa5b7584205ae22fd110fdce7d1)

385.

Some butterflies can have both male and female characteristics, with one colorful wing and one plain wing.

Reference: (https://en.wikipedia.org/wiki/Gynandromorphism)

386.

To clean up after using the lavatory, ancient Romans used a "tersorium", a sponge on the end of a long stick that was shared by everyone in the community. When not in use, the stick stayed in a bucket of vinegar or seawater in the communal bathroom.

Reference: (https://www.sapiens.org/column/curiosities/ancient-roman-bathrooms/)

387.

The pike with cars impaled on it, as seen in the Bohemian Rhapsody scene in "Wayne's World," was a controversial art installation titled "Spindle." It was demolished in 2008.

Reference: (https://en.wikipedia.org/wiki/Spindle_(sculpture))

388.

Jackie Kennedy was a polyglot, mastered French and speaking also some German and Italian as well as Spanish fluently. She taped radio ads in French, Italian and Spanish, urging the listeners to vote for her husband.

Reference: (http://www.americathebilingual.com/jackie-kennedys-prowess-as-a-polygot/)

389.

Thomas Nichols, brother of Nichelle Nichols, Uhura in the original "Star Trek," died in the religious mass suicide of the Heaven's Gate group.

Reference: (https://en.wikipedia.org/wiki/Heaven%27s_Gate_(religious_group))

390.

The Benz Velo, introduced in 1894, participated in the world's first automobile race. Rather than fastest time, the automobiles would be judged on whether they were safe and cost effective to operate.

Reference: (https://en.wikipedia.org/wiki/Benz_Velo)

391.

Sacagawea was instrumental in the success of the Lewis and Clark Expedition and received no compensation for her contributions as a guide and Shoshone interpreter. She was a teen with a 2 month old baby when she started the journey to discovering the western United States after the Louisiana Purchase.

Reference: (https://www.shessocoolpod.com/podcast-1/episode/f16949f8/sacagawea)

392.

In 1903, Ford advertised its Model A as the "most reliable machine in the world" and the success of this car model generated a profit for the Ford Motor Company when it had only $223.65 left in its bank account,

Reference: (https://en.wikipedia.org/wiki/Ford_Model_A_(1903%E2%80%9304))

393.

The creator of Rudolph The Red Nosed Reindeer was Jewish and identified with the underdog Rudolph because of his prominent nose.

Reference:(https://www.thedailybeast.com/how-a-shy-jewish-boys-nose-issues-gave-america-rudolf-for-christmas)

394.

Wyoming and Colorado both have a mean elevation that is higher than the tallest Appalachian "mountain" Mt. Mitchell.

Reference: (https://www.netstate.com/states/tables/state_elevation_mean.htm)

395.

About half of all vegetables are grown in China.

Reference: (https://en.wikipedia.org/wiki/Vegetable#Top_producers)

396.

Ghana was one of the richest nations in Africa at the time of independence in 1957. By 1965, it had become virtually bankrupt due to massive corruption and the centralization of decision-making in the hands of its leader, who often signed multimillion-dollar contracts without informing anyone.

Reference: (http://www.orwelltoday.com/africahistory.shtml)

397.

Because of census fraud, regional rivalries and the aid agencies' own tendency to overstatement, we still do not even know if the population figure we use for Africa, 800 million, is accurate.

Reference:(https://www.independent.co.uk/arts-entertainment/books/reviews/the-state-of-africa-by-martin-meredith-297541.html)

398.

The actress who starred as the orphan in the 1982 film "Annie" now heads a swing band called Aileen Quinn and the Leapin' Lizards.

Reference: (http://www.aileenquinnandtheleapinlizards.com/)

399.

The females of a type of horse fly doesn't suck blood. Pollen grains found on the face of museum specimens suggest that they visit flowers and pollinate instead.

Reference: (https://bugguide.net/node/view/1491298)

400.

Cotard Delusion, also known as Walking Corpse Syndrome, is a neurological and psychiatric disorder in which the affected person may see their own face but not perceive it as themselves, leading them to believe that they themselves do not exist.

Reference: (https://en.wikipedia.org/wiki/Cotard_delusion)

401.

Europeans actually used to eat Egyptian mummies.

Reference: (https://www.historyanswers.co.uk/news/the-europeans-that-ate-egyptian-mummies/)

402.

In the 1940s and 1950s, hundreds of thousands of members of the U.S. armed forces were exposed to ionizing radiation from nuclear testing during active duty. These "atomic veterans" were sworn to secrecy, and many received no treatment or compensation for the illnesses they later developed.

Reference: (https://www.nytimes.com/2019/02/12/opinion/atomic-soldiers.html)

403.

The Statue of Liberty's hand sat in Madison Square park for 6 years before being installed. While the French paid for the statue, the U.S. didn't want to pay for the pedestal, so to raise money, photographs were sold to tourists and for 50 cents, you could climb a ladder to the top of the torch.

Reference:(https://vinepair.com/cocktail-chatter/statue-of-liberty-hand/)

404.

Sauternes is a white wine made with grapes infected by a fungus known as "noble rot," which causes the grapes to raisin on the vine, sweetening the end result. They traditionally ferment in barrels in which a sulfur-dipped candle was burned, to inhibit yeast and increase residual sugars.

Reference: (https://en.wikipedia.org/wiki/Sauternes_(wine))

405.

There are over 30 schools around the world, called "Sudbury Schools" which are run as complete democracies. The students and staff share equal votes on hiring and firing staff, as well as use of school budget and school rules.

Reference: (https://en.wikipedia.org/wiki/Sudbury_school#School_democracy)

406.

The U.S. may have adopted the metric system if pirates hadn't kidnapped Joseph Dombey, the French scientist sent to help Thomas Jefferson persuade Congress to adopt the system.

Reference: (https://www.nist.gov/blogs/taking-measure/pirates-caribbean-metric-edition)

407.

The lawsuit versus Subway for selling 11 inch footlong subs was thrown out. While most people think of this as Subway short changing customers, the reality was that there was no difference in food by weight.

Reference:(https://www.reuters.com/article/us-subway-decision-footlong/worthless-subway-footlong-sandwich-settlement-is-thrown-out-u-s-court-idUSKCN1B52H6)

408.

"Egyptian" cotton is actually native to Peru and Ecuador.

Reference: (https://en.wikipedia.org/wiki/Gossypium_barbadense)

409.

The word "shmoo" is a technical term with different meanings in the fields of electrical engineering, cell biology, socioeconomics, echinoderm biology, and particle physics. In all these cases, the term is a reference to the Shmoo, a cartoon animal from the comic strip Li'l Abner.

Reference: (https://en.wikipedia.org/wiki/Shmoo#In_science)

410.

In Formula One, from 2010, refuelling is no longer permitted during the race.

Reference: (https://en.wikipedia.org/wiki/Formula_One_regulations)

411.

Disposable face masks are worn blue-side out, and white-side in.

Reference:(https://www.sfcdcp.org/communicable-disease/healthy-habits/how-to-put-on-and-remove-a-face-mask/)

412.

Citizens of Moscow receive their hot water from a series of plants throughout the city, which is shut down temporarily in the summer months for maintenance.

Reference: (https://www.nytimes.com/2007/08/21/world/europe/21moscow.html)

413.

Jef Raskin, who started the Macintosh project, resigned his associate professorship at the University of California in San Diego by flying over the Chancellor's residence with a hot air balloon, yelled down he's resigning, and floated off.

Reference: (https://www.zdnet.com/article/minority-report-jef-raskin-and-the-mac-revolution/)

414.

"The Return of the King" of the Lord of the Rings movie trilogy was nominated for 11 academy awards. It won in every single category it was nominated for.

Reference:(https://en.wikipedia.org/wiki/List_of_accolades_received_by_The_Lord_of_the_Rings_film_series)

415.

Wealthy ancient Romans would purchase Portuguese urine, believed to contain more ammonia than other urine, and use it as a mouthwash. Urine remained a popular ingredient in mouthwash until the 18th century.

Reference:(https://www.pediatricdentalcare.com/blog/the-crazy-and-disgusting-history-of-mouthwash/)

416.

King Willem-Alexander of the Netherlands is 889th in line to the British throne.

Reference:(https://www.theguardian.com/world/2013/apr/30/king-willem-12-things-dutch-royal-family)

417.

"All My Life" by Foo Fighters is about Dave Grohl's love of performing oral sex on women.

Reference: (https://en.wikipedia.org/wiki/All_My_Life_(Foo_Fighters_song))

418.

Stefan Lux, a Czech reporter, committed suicide on the floor of the League of Nations to bring attention to the dangers of Nazi Germany.

Reference: (https://en.wikipedia.org/wiki/%C5%A0tefan_Lux)

419.

Jerome Flynn, the actor behind Ser Bronn in "Game of Thrones," sang in a 1990's cover band called Robson & Jerome.

Reference: (https://www.youtube.com/watch?v=r5V8ecsrxeY)

420.

At 211 days, a man named "Bonar Law" was the shortest serving U.K. Prime Minister of the 20th century. Some New Brunswick teenagers get the privilege of attending "Bonar Law Memorial High School."

Reference: (https://en.wikipedia.org/wiki/Bonar_Law)

421.

Jacksonville, Florida is west of all of South America.

Reference: (http://www.somethinggeography.com/2016/10/where-is-south-america.html?m=1)

422.

John C. Fremont, the first Republican nominee for president, was pardoned by James K. Polk after being convicted for mutiny.

Reference:(https://www.deseretnews.com/article/865646853/This-week-in-history-John-C-Frmont-is-court-martialed-for-mutiny.html)

423.

"Mad honey" is a honey made by bees gathering pollen from rhododendrons.

Reference: (https://www.inverse.com/article/33974-mad-honey-rhododendron-grayanotoxin)

424.

The Verve have never made a penny from their song "Bitter Sweet Symphony".

Reference: (https://www.bbc.com/news/entertainment-arts-48380600)

425.

Thomas Howard, 3rd Duke of Norfolk, was due to be executed on the January 29, 1547, but his life was spared when Henry VIII died the day before.

Reference:(https://en.wikipedia.org/wiki/Thomas_Howard,_3rd_Duke_of_Norfolk#Imprisonment_and_release)

426.

In India, white people are an officially recognized minority and are assigned two members in the Lok Sabha (Indian Parliament).

Reference: (https://en.wikipedia.org/wiki/Anglo-Indian#Political_status)

427.

A public high school in Alabama consistently ranks as one of the best in the country and has been ranked number 1.

Reference:(https://en.wikipedia.org/wiki/Jefferson_County_International_Baccalaureate_School)

428.

The King of Siam used to gift albino elephants to courtiers who displeased him, in order to ruin them with the upkeep costs. This is the supposed inspiration for the White Elephant Gift Exchange.

Reference: (https://en.wikipedia.org/wiki/White_elephant_gift_exchange)

429.

Warsaw Shore is a Jersey Shore spinoff that has been running since 2013 and has 11 seasons.

Reference: (https://en.wikipedia.org/wiki/Warsaw_Shore)

430.

New BAND-AID bandages are made from touch screen-friendly material.

Reference:(https://www.jnj.com/our-heritage/18-facts-about-the-history-of-band-aid-brand-adhesive-bandages)

431.

Jaguar XF's start button pulses at the rate of 72 BPM, which is the heart rate of a resting jaguar cat.

Reference: (https://www.jaguar.com/jaguar-range/xf/features/interior.html)

432.

The director of "Kubo and the Two Strings," Travis Knight, is the son of the founder of Nike and was once a rapper by the name of "Chilly Tee".

Reference: (https://www.youtube.com/watch?v=McWU6N_PdV4)

433.

Mike Tyson declared bankruptcy in the year 2003 despite having earned over $300 million throughout his boxing career; he had $23 million in debt.

Reference: (https://en.wikipedia.org/wiki/Mike_Tyson)

434.

Exo cannibals eat people from outside their social group, while endo cannibals eat members of their own community.

Reference: (https://en.wikipedia.org/wiki/Exocannibalism)

435.

In 1993, Bruce Lee's son Brandon was fatally shot and killed by a "dummy round" on the set of his movie "The Crow". The homemade dummy bullets were exchanged for real blanks due to safety reasons but one dummy was left in the chamber.

Reference: (https://en.wikipedia.org/wiki/Brandon_Lee)

436.

The famous "Hollywood" sign is spelled out in 45-foot tall letters and is 352 feet long. The sign was originally created in 1923 as an advertisement for a local real estate development, but due to increasing recognition, was left up.

Reference: (https://en.wikipedia.org/wiki/Hollywood_Sign)

437.

From 1993 to 1998, Joseph Parvin of Lawrenceville, New Jersey managed to obtain 26,554 compact discs using the introductory offers from BMG Music Services and Columbia House Music Club. The CDs were addressed to 2,417 customer accounts and delivered to 16 P.O. boxes and his home address.

Reference:(https://www.nytimes.com/2000/03/25/nyregion/man-admits-fraud-in-joining-cd-clubs-thousands-of-times.html?fbclid=IwAR13thbsSN3dVi_rKpl9fHFKNk7lIOlhWnhdE5m0BQ9e9kf2pJm9blN-jak)

438.

The Donner Party ate each other, brewed soup out of bones and shunned other families kids whose parents left to find help like 2nd class humans because they decided to take a "faster" route through the Sierra Nevada Mountains.

Reference: (https://www.history.com/news/10-things-you-should-know-about-the-donner-party)

439.

Despite its positive reception, "Matilda" failed to make back its budget at the U.S. box office.

Reference: (https://en.wikipedia.org/wiki/Matilda_(1996_film)#Box_office)

440.

Emmanuel Quaye, who played Strika in "The Beasts of No Nation", is begging in the streets of Ghana as he never received any money paid directly to him. A supposed fund with $30,000 is supposedly waiting for him when he turns 18. He has no paperwork of this.

Reference: (https://allafrica.com/stories/201808220077.html)

441.

Actor Pat Roach had two different roles in "Indiana Jones and the Raiders of the Lost Ark", he also happened to be the British and European heavyweight wrestling champion.

Reference: (https://nothingbutnostalgia.com/raiders-of-the-lost-ark-cast/)

442.

Prague had not one, but two historic defenestrations. The second one, where 2 Catholics were thrown out of a 21 meter high window sparked a 30 year long war. The two men survived. According to Catholics, they were caught by the Virgin Mary, while Protestants say they just fell into a dung pile.

Reference: (https://www.atlasobscura.com/places/defenestration-of-prague-window)

443.

Lovebugs are an actual insect found near the Gulf of Mexico. They got their name because adult pairs remain attached for several days during mating.

Reference: (https://en.wikipedia.org/wiki/Lovebug)

444.

After you die, your brain knows you're dead.

Reference:(https://nypost.com/2017/10/19/after-you-die-your-brain-knows-youre-dead-terrifying-study-reveals/)

445.

The famed poet Lord Byron was disabled. He was born with a clubbed foot, and walked with a halting gait. Byron went to great lengths to hide and overcompensate for his disability, and poured himself into his poetry, using it as an emotional outlet.

Reference:(https://www.hands-free.co.uk/deformed-transformed-lord-byrons-disability-inspired-poetry/)

446.

Ferdinand Porsche invented the first gasoline and electric hybrid and remained committed to the technology throughout his life; the Elephant tank destroyer, also known as the "Ferdinand" in World War II, had a hybrid drivetrain.

Reference: (http://www.hybrid-vehicle.org/hybrid-vehicle-porsche.html)

447.

Erskine Hamilton Childers, who was the first Protestant President of Ireland, and the son of Erskine Childers, a famous author, was executed during the Irish Civil War.

Reference: (https://en.wikipedia.org/wiki/Erskine_Hamilton_Childers)

448.

Japanese performance artist Mao Sugiyama cooked his genitals with mushrooms and parsley, and served it to 5 individuals that had paid 100,000 yen each. Japanese authorities were notified but chose not to act, as cannibalism is not illegal in Japan.

Reference:(https://www.huffingtonpost.ca/2012/05/24/asexual-mao-sugiyama-cooks-serves-own-genitals_n_1543307.html)

449.

President Ronald Reagan had a stack of index cards with one-liner jokes on them. He kept it in his desk in the Oval Office, and would insert the lines into speeches to help them go over well.

Reference: (https://www.youtube.com/watch?v=HA7sP47e8tA)

450.

The film "The Darkest Minds" had the largest theatre drop of all time. It lost 2,679 theatres in its second week, dropping from 3,127 to 448.

Reference: (https://www.boxofficemojo.com/alltime/theaterdrops.htm)

451.

Richard L. McKinley died in a nuclear plant accident. His body ended so contaminated that it had to be buried in a lead-lined casket, which was then sealed in concrete and placed in a metal vault and cannot be moved from its location without the approval of the Atomic Energy Commission.

Reference: (http://www.arlingtoncemetery.net/rlmckinl.htm)

452.

In 2002, after having smoked PCP, Big Lurch was found naked and covered with blood; it was soon discovered he had in his stomach bits of flesh and lungs from Tynisha Ysais, his friend's girlfriend who was found dead. He was sentenced to life without parole for murdering her.

Reference: (https://en.wikipedia.org/wiki/Big_Lurch#Murder_and_lawsuit)

453.

Former professional baseball catcher Jorge Posada never wore gloves and used to urinate on his hands to make them tougher, a practice he stopped after his wife found out.

Reference: (http://archive.boston.com/sports/baseball/articles/2011/09/23/glove_story/)

454.

Ann Arbor, Michigan once had a volunteer hippie police force called the "Psychedelic Rangers".

Reference: (https://aadl.org/node/195895)

455.

Ziona Chana is the head of the world's largest family, with 39 wives, 94 children, 14 daughters-in-law and 33 grandchildren, 180 in total and counting.

Reference: (https://en.wikipedia.org/wiki/Ziona)

456.

Sloths are better swimmers than they are climbers.

Reference: (https://roaring.earth/sloths-swim/)

457.

After surviving starvation with the Donner Party, Mary Graves married a man who was soon murdered. She cooked his murderer meals in prison so that he would not starve before his execution.

Reference: (https://en.wikipedia.org/wiki/Donner_Party#Survivors)

458.

The term "fedora" is derived from the Greek name "Theodora" which means "God's gift".

Reference: (https://www.sheknows.com/baby-names/name/fedora/)

459.

The fig remnants in a deceased person's stomach grew into a tree, which helped authorities to identify where missing people were buried.

Reference:(http://www.hurriyetdailynews.com/how-a-fig-tree-helped-to-identify-a-slain-turkish-cypriot-in-search-of-missing-persons-in-divided-cyprus-136986)

460.

Éamon de Valera, President of Ireland, was made an honorary chief of the Ojibwe-Chippewa people, in 1919 in Wisconsin.

Reference: (https://ansionnachfionn.com/2014/03/12/the-irish-revolution-and-native-america/)

461.

Isabelline animals, unlike albinos which completely lack pigment, are just super light in pigment.

Reference: (https://www.strangebio.com/post/115909141909/isabelline-animals-as-beautiful-as-their-name)

462.

In 1936, Pennsylvania placed a "temporary" tax on all alcohol sales to help out victims of the Johnstown Flood, and that tax is still charged.

Reference: (https://www.ydr.com/story/news/2017/04/12/pas-18-hidden-tax-supposed-temporary-1936/100343742/)

463.

David Bowie did not suffer from heterochromia. Rather, he had a condition known as anisocoria, where one pupil is permanently more dilated than the other, as a result of a fistfight with a friend in his youth. That friend was George Underwood, his lifelong artistic partner.

Reference: (https://www.thecut.com/2016/01/story-behind-david-bowies-unusual-eyes.html)

464.

The balcony in Romeo and Juliet doesn't exist. It's not in the original play and was picked up from another author's play and inserted into Shakespeare's story about 100 years later. Shakespeare simply has Juliet standing by a window.

Reference: (https://www.theatlantic.com/entertainment/archive/2014/10/romeo-and-juliets-balcony-scene-doesnt-exist/381969/)

465.

India has Autonomous Administrative Divisions which are provided with varying degrees of Autonomy based on Sixth Schedule of Indian Constitution.

Reference: (https://en.wikipedia.org/wiki/Autonomous_administrative_divisions_of_India)

466.

When building the Central Pacific Railroad, the 75-degree slope of the American River Gorge was considered impossible. Chinese workers wove baskets to lower men from the cliff tops to do the blasting.

Reference: (https://www.historynet.com/working-railroad-chinese-way.htm)

467.

Dr. Christopher Duntsch is a neurosurgeon who was tried, convicted and sentenced to life in prison for gross malpractice due to killing two patients and maiming four others.

Reference: (https://en.wikipedia.org/wiki/Christopher_Duntsch)

468.

Saturn's moons Janus and Epimetheus swap orbits every 4 years or so.

Reference: (http://planetary.org/blogs/emily-lakdawalla/2006/janus-epimetheus-swap.html)

469.

A schizophrenic programmer named Terry Davis would upload videos online claiming to be the greatest programmer. In his last video uploaded hours before his death he says, "Wait, maybe. I think maybe I'm just like a little bizarre little person who walks back and forth. Whatever, you know."

Reference: (https://en.wikipedia.org/wiki/Terry_A._Davis)

470.

A family has been passing down a pickle in a jar since 1876.

Reference:(https://www.npr.org/2011/10/09/141167586/florida-family-s-legacy-135-year-old-pickle)

471.

The development of the first credit card was accredited to Frank McNamara in 1950. He wanted to create a card of credit for faithful patrons of his restaurant. Eventually, American Express picked up the idea and created the universal entertainment and travel card.

Reference: (https://www.britannica.com/topic/credit-card)

472.

The North Hollywood Medical Center, where "Scrubs" was filmed, was also the site of filming for scenes from "Malcolm in the Middle," "Charmed," and "The Sopranos." It was demolished in mid-2011.

Reference: (https://en.wikipedia.org/wiki/North_Hollywood_Medical_Center)

473.

There was a radio program in Havana in the 1960s called "Radio Free Dixie" aimed at African Americans. It played Soul Music and news. It reached the entire continental U.S.

Reference: (https://en.wikipedia.org/wiki/Radio_Free_Dixie)

474.

The Onagawa Nuclear Power Plant survived the same earthquake and tsunami that destroyed Fukushima while being closer to the epicenter. In fact, it was used as a shelter afterwards

Reference:(https://en.wikipedia.org/w/index.php?title=Onagawa_Nuclear_Power_Plant&action=edit&section=5)

475.

A national test in South Korea is so extreme that students can be escorted to take the exam by the police if they're running late.

Reference: (https://en.wikipedia.org/wiki/College_Scholastic_Ability_Test)

476.

In 1974, British Leyland made a car so bad that a magazine article about that single car's faults spread internationally. It was a Rover 3500 that consumed 3 engines, 2 gearboxes, 2 clutch housings and a set of electrical cables in 6000 miles, having spent over two thirds of its time in the workshop.

Reference: (https://en.wikipedia.org/wiki/Rover_P6#Series_II)

477.

In the "Terminator 2" movie Linda Hamilton's double was played by her twin sister Leslie.

Reference: (https://terminator.fandom.com/wiki/Leslie_Hamilton_Gearren)

478.

In 2012, a physicist faced with a fine for running a stop sign, proved his innocence by publishing a mathematical paper.

Reference: (https://www.businessinsider.com/dmitri-krioukov-avoids-traffic-ticket-2012-4)

479.

Capsaicin, he active ingredient in hot peppers, is similar to vanillin, in vanilla.

Reference: (https://justenoughheat.com/education/behind-the-burn/)

480.

Gabe Mirkin, the man responsible for coining the acronym RICE, rest, ice, compression, and elevation, a mnemonic for treatment of soft tissue injuries, recanted his support for the regimen in 2014, saying that ice and complete rest may delay healing.

Reference: (https://en.wikipedia.org/wiki/RICE_(medicine))

481.

Saint George's Cross comes from the Italian city of Genoa. The English government paid the Genoese to use their flag in 1190, as they had a reputation for driving away pirates. This became the permanent flag of England.

Reference: (https://en.wikipedia.org/wiki/Saint_George%27s_Cross)

482.

Machine learning can generate realistic "videos" of talking heads from a few photos.

Reference: (https://www.youtube.com/watch?v=p1b5aiTrGzY&amp=&feature=share)

483.

Tom Barry fought in World War I as a captain in the British forces. He then went on to lead one of the most successful flying columns of the IRA in the fight for Irish independence. Outmanned over 10:1 and massively out gunned, he lead a guerrilla campaign which eventually drove the British out.

Reference: (https://en.wikipedia.org/wiki/Tom_Barry_(Irish_republican))

484.

All plants of the same stock of bamboo will bloom at the same time, and then die, no matter where they are in the world. Usually once every hundred years or so.

Reference: (https://grapee.jp/en/114838)

485.

Keanu Reeves had two female stalkers enter his home within three days of each other in 2014.

Reference: (https://www.thewrap.com/naked-female-intruder-invades-keanu-reeves-home/)

486.

Bees have two stomachs, one stomach for eating and the other special stomach is for storing nectar collected from flowers or water so that they can carry it back to their hive.

Reference: (https://www.ontariohoney.ca/kids-zone/bee-facts)

487.

Tobacco is more addicting than pure nicotine because tobacco smoke has MAOi's in it.

Reference: (https://www.ncbi.nlm.nih.gov/m/pubmed/16177026/)

488.

The SS Princess Alice, a paddleboat steamer, sank in the river Thames in 1878, killing upwards of 700 people, many of whom died from ingesting the heavily raw sewage and industrial waste polluted waters of the river.

Reference: (https://en.wikipedia.org/wiki/Sinking_of_SS_Princess_Alice)

489.

The estranged wife from "Die Hard," actress Bonnie Bedelia is the aunt of Macaulay Culkin.

Reference: (https://en.wikipedia.org/wiki/Bonnie_Bedelia)

490.

Cockroaches wouldn't actually survive a nuclear blast.

Reference:(https://pursuit.unimelb.edu.au/articles/would-cockroaches-really-survive-a-nuclear-apocalypse?utm_source=twiter&utm_medium=social&utm_content=story)

491.

The first U.S. airship disaster happened because the balloon was so big and its shape so strange that the pilots couldn't hear the orders of their captain. It wobbled and collapsed injuring 16 people.

Reference: (https://todayinsci.com/Events/Aircraft/MorrellAirship-Collapse.htm)

492.

A military psychology tactic in late World War II was to attach whistles on bombs. As the bombs fell, they made the terrifying decrescendo whistling sound we think of today. The same sound is often dubbed over every type of bomb in movies and cartoons, despite only being used on a few specific bombs.

Reference: (https://en.wikipedia.org/wiki/Stuka#Ju_87B)

493.

In 1998, Enron built and maintained a completely fake trading floor on the 6th floor of their headquarters to impress Wall St. analysts.

Reference: (https://www.theguardian.com/business/2002/feb/21/corporatefraud.enron1)

494.

After a Polish nobleman converted to Judaism and was burned at the stake for apostasy, the town that had provided the firewood burned down and a nearby building blackened by smoke was torn down after repeated attempts to paint over the stain failed to cover it.

Reference: (https://en.wikipedia.org/wiki/Abraham_ben_Abraham)

495.

Craig Mazin, writer and creator of the dark and disturbing HBO miniseries, Chernobyl, was previously known only as a comedy creator who wrote movies such as Superhero Movie, Scary Movie 3, and The Hangover Parts II and III.

Reference: (https://en.wikipedia.org/wiki/Craig_Mazin)

496.

When Bob Marley first presented his last album to Chris Blackwell, Blackwell told him it was missing something. Next day Bob Marley came back with an addition to the album, "Redemption Song".

Reference:(https://www.independent.co.uk/arts-entertainment/music/features/story-of-the-song-bob-marleys-redemption-song-2003143.html)

497.

The elaeomyxa cerifera is an iridescent purple fungi which bursts open and releases spores that look like glitter.

Reference:(https://www.abc.net.au/news/2018-11-26/slime-mould-tasmania-fungi-hunting/10554338)

498.

Alexander Thynn is the 7th Marquess of Bath. He is a British peer who paints erotic scenes from the Kama Sutra on the walls of his estate, has openly had sexual relations with over seventy women during his marriage, many of them live in estate cottages, and he refers to them as wifelets.

Reference: (https://en.wikipedia.org/wiki/Alexander_Thynn,_7th_Marquess_of_Bath)

499.

Water Buffalo milk is a 38 billion dollar industry; making it more valuable than apples, bananas and coffee individually.

Reference: (https://en.wikipedia.org/wiki/List_of_most_valuable_crops_and_livestock_products)

500.

50 Cent briefly considered getting involved in the mining industry. He met with a South African billionaire and considered purchasing an equity stake in a platinum mine shaft in the hopes of launching his own branded line of platinum.

Reference: (https://en.wikipedia.org/wiki/50_Cent)

501.

There is a functional link between syphilis and the popularity of codpieces in the 1500s. Syphilis showed up in Europe in 1494 shortly after Columbus returned and codpieces appeared around 1500. The codpiece protected the penis, held medicinal ointments and protected stylish clothing.

Reference: (https://daily.jstor.org/the-codpiece-and-the-pox/)

502.

In 2013, police in the Maldives arrested a coconut for loitering near a polling station for the presidential election. Locals feared the coconut may have been imbued with a black magic spell to influence the election as there was a Surah written on it.

Reference:(https://www.theguardian.com/world/2013/sep/06/coconut-detained-maldives-vote-rigging)

503.

The Solar Storm of 1859 was a powerful geomagnetic storm that caused telegraph systems all over Europe and North America to fail, in some cases giving telegraph operators electric shocks.

Reference: (https://en.wikipedia.org/wiki/Solar_storm_of_1859)

504.

The character Leela in "Futurama" was named after the Turangalîla-Symphonie by Olivier Messiaen.

Reference: (https://en.wikipedia.org/wiki/Leela_(Futurama)#Conception)

505.

Medieval historians have found evidence that a nun in the 14th century faked her own death and crafted a dummy "in the likeness of her body" in order to escape her convent and pursue, in the words of the archbishop of the time, "the way of carnal lust".

Reference:(https://www.theguardian.com/books/2019/feb/11/archive-shows-medieval-nun-faked-her-own-death-to-escape-convent)

506.

Nurses use a slang word "Hasselhoff" meaning, patients who come to the emergency room with injuries that are just bizarre. It came from David Hasselhoff which is a Baywatch actor. He went to the hospital with a severed artery in his arm and four tendons after getting hit by a chandelier while he's shaving.

Reference: (https://www.nursebuff.com/medical-slang/)

507.

Karen Greenlee is the best-known modern practitioner of necrophilia.

Reference: (https://en.wikipedia.org/wiki/Karen_Greenlee)

508.

There is no evidence for the widely-believed claim that Victorian doctors used vibrators to treat hysteria.

Reference:(http://journalofpositivesexuality.org/wp-content/uploads/2018/08/Failure-of-Academic-Quality-Control-Technology-of-Orgasm-Lieberman-Schatzberg.pdf)

509.

A mass of Cornium, lava created due to nuclear core meltdown, called The Elephant's foot, can kill you with only 300 seconds of exposure, serious cell damage with only 2 minutes and cause dizziness in 30 seconds.

Reference: (http://nautil.us/blog/chernobyls-hot-mess-the-elephants-foot-is-still-lethal)

510.

The word "zenzizenzizenzic" was coined in the 16th century to represent the 8th power of a number.

Reference: (https://en.wikipedia.org/wiki/Zenzizenzizenzic)

511.

During the shooting of the music video for the Dokken classic "Dream Warriors", the band did cocaine with Robert England. England was dressed up in full Freddy attire including his trademark razor glove, which he used to serve bumps of cocaine on for the entire band.

Reference:(https://www.dreadcentral.com/news/285032/that-time-robert-englund-dokken-did-cocaine-off-freddy-kruegers-glove/)

512.

The Silurian hypothesis is a thought experiment which assesses modern science's ability to detect evidence of a prior advanced civilization, perhaps several million years ago. The author pondered whether it would "be possible to detect an industrial civilization in the geological record?"

Reference: (https://en.wikipedia.org/wiki/Silurian_hypothesis)

513.

The children's song "The Hokey Cokey" is only called this in the U.K., Ireland and the Caribbean, while it's called "The Hokey Pokey" in the U.S., Canada, Australia and Israel as 3 similar songs were released within an 11 year period with no one knowing who originally wrote the song we know now.

Reference:(http://www.bbcamerica.com/anglophenia/2012/03/frasers-phrases-the-curious-history-of-the-hokey-cokey)

514.

The German submarine U-1206 was lost due to a toilet malfunction: the leak flooded the submarine's batteries causing them to release chlorine gas, leaving the Commander with no alternative but to surface. Once surfaced, U-1206 was discovered and bombed by British patrols.

Reference: (https://en.wikipedia.org/wiki/German_submarine_U-1206)

515.

Some parents give their kids bleach to "cure autism". This, of course, does not work.

Reference:(https://www.healthline.com/health-news/parents-warned-about-bleach-therapy-for-autism#2)

516.

Laundry detergent only removes stains and doesn't kill germs or bacteria. Only washing in hot water with bleach kills them. Washing clothes in cold water just spreads the germs around the clothes.

Reference: (https://www.ncbi.nlm.nih.gov/pmc/articles/PMC4672060/)

517.

The Papal election of 1268 to 1271 was the longest in history. It took so long that while the cardinals were locked in, their rations were reduced to bread and water, the roof of their hall was removed, and 3 died of old age. The new Pope changed the rules to stop it from repeating, making the Conclave.

Reference: (https://en.wikipedia.org/wiki/1268%E2%80%9371_papal_election)

518.

In Bunce Island, Sierra Leone, scottish slavers built their own golf course on the island and dressed their slave caddies in tartan.

Reference:(https://www.heraldscotland.com/news/17200038.how-slavery-made-the-modern-scotland/)

519.

Grapes are poisonous to dogs.

Reference: (https://www.akc.org/expert-advice/nutrition/can-dogs-eat-grapes/)

520.

Richard Burton, after portraying Winston Churchill, was permanently banned from the BBC after criticizing Churchill's alleged promise to wipe out all Japanese people on the planet.

Reference: (https://en.wikipedia.org/wiki/Richard_Burton)

521.

Genuine ideas to raise RMS Titanic from the sea bed included filling it with vaseline or ping pong balls, as well as turning the ship into an iceberg itself so it would float to the surface.

Reference:(https://en.wikipedia.org/wiki/Wreck_of_the_RMS_Titanic#Salvage_proposals_in_the_1960s_and_1970s)

522.

Western Xia was the only nation that stopped Genghis Khan and the man was killed in combat with Western Xia. However, the nation suffered a tragic genocide by his successors per Genghis Khan's will.

Reference: (https://www.history.com/this-day-in-history/genghis-khan-dies)

523.

When Bruce Springsteen was 19, he dodged his army draft by behaving "crazily" during the induction and not writing anything in tests. He later went on to write the song "Born in the USA" which was the singer's reflection on the plight of American veterans returning home from Vietnam.

Reference: (https://www.history.com/this-day-in-history/genghis-khan-dies)

524.

Split peas were used to compare rivets in the manufacture of Supermarine Spitfire fighter aircrafts.

Reference: (https://en.wikipedia.org/wiki/Split_pea#Culinary_uses)

525.

Dave Mirra, professional BMX Rider and Rally Racer with 14 gold medals in BMX competitions, committed suicide on February 14, 2016. He was posthumously diagnosed with Chronic Traumatic Encephalopathy, a neurodegenerative disease caused by repeated brain injuries.

Reference: (https://en.wikipedia.org/wiki/Dave_Mirra)

526.

First Lady Jackie Kennedy was unimpressed by the palace furnishings and by the Queen's dress and hairstyle following a meeting in 1961. Jackie, working as the Inquiring Camera Girl for the Washington-Times Herald, covered Elizabeth's coronation almost a decade earlier.

Reference:(https://www.vanityfair.com/hollywood/2017/12/queen-elizabeth-jackie-kennedy-the-crown-netflix)

527.

The Louisiana Maneuvers were a series of war games held a few months before Pearl Harbor. They centered around a conflict between two fictional countries, Kotmk and Almat. The army of Almat won, thanks primarily to the efforts of General George S. Patton.

Reference:(https://en.wikipedia.org/wiki/Louisiana_Maneuvers)

528.

The original Scooby Doo story treatment had Shaggy as Velma's brother, Scooby Doo was a bongo playing dog named Too Much, and they were a band who solved mysteries when not playing gigs.

Reference: (https://en.wikipedia.org/wiki/Scooby-Doo#Development)

529.

USSR-aligned countries were forced to refuse the Marshall Plan, in which the U.S. gave billions of dollars in economic assistance to help rebuild EU economies after the end of World War II.

Reference: (https://www.history.com/topics/world-war-ii/marshall-plan-1)

530.

Matt Damon started writing "Good Will Hunting" as a final assignment for a playwriting class he was taking at Harvard University. At first, it was written as a thriller about a young man who possesses a superior intelligence and is targeted by the government with heavy-handed recruitment.

Reference: (https://en.wikipedia.org/wiki/Good_Will_Hunting)

531.

Harvard Economics professor Stephen Marglin was a prodigy within in his field, received tenure at a young age and then immediately published papers calling for the abolishment of capitalism. Vox called it one of the greatest pranks in the history of academia.

Reference:(https://www.thecrimson.com/article/1980/3/12/stephen-marglin-pbonce-the-jewel-of/)

532.

Brushing your teeth after orange juice actually hurts your teeth.

Reference:(https://www.drinkbai.com/blog/health-and-wellness/why-juice-tastes-so-bad-after-you-brush-your-teeth)

533.

The planet Vormir, which appeared in "Avengers: Infinity War" and "Avengers: Endgame", is based on the scenery of Lençóis Maranhenses National Park, Brazil.

Reference:(https://en.wikipedia.org/wiki/Len%C3%A7%C3%B3is_Maranhenses_National_Park)

534.

Bart Simpson's middle name is JoJo.

Reference: (https://en.wikipedia.org/wiki/Bart_Simpson)

535.

In 2001, a pair of astronomers managed to find the average colour of the universe, describing it as a "Cosmic Latte".

Reference:(https://en.wikipedia.org/wiki/Cosmic_latte)

536.

In 1994, Frito-Lay spent $50 million on research and development for changing the Dorito to have rounded corners and be 20% larger.

Reference: (https://en.wikipedia.org/wiki/Doritos)

537.

There is a flame at a Zoroastrian fire temple in Iran that has supposedly been burning continuously since the year 470.

Reference: (https://en.wikipedia.org/wiki/Yazd_Atash_Behram#History)

538.

In 1929, Princeton researchers opened a cat's skull and connected the auditory nerve to a telephone. When one researcher spoke in the cat's ear, the other could hear it through the receiver 50 feet away. The experiment ultimately became the basis for cochlear implants. year 470.

Reference: (https://blogs.princeton.edu/mudd/2017/04/the-cat-telephone/)

539.

A study in 1978 tested the success of asking to cut in line to use a copy machine. When no reason was given, 60% of those asked agreed. When adding, "because I'm in a rush" 94% agreed. Though the reason mattered little, as even with, "because I have to make copies," 93% of those asked agreed.

Reference:(https://www.researchgate.net/publication/232505985_The_mindlessness_of_ostensibly_thoughtful_action_The_role_of_placebic_information_in_interpersonal_interaction)

540.

There was an Arcade version of Super Mario World, using the Nintendo Super System.

Reference:(https://www.giantbomb.com/nintendo-super-system/3015-3204/)

541.

In U.S. elections, a voter can write the name of any one they want in the ballot. This is called "write in" and it is even valid in many states. Mickey Mouse is U.S. most favourite "write in" candidate.

Reference: (https://www.bbc.com/news/election-us-2016-37626319)

542.

Paper Straws were invented in the 1880s because Marvin Stone hated the gritty residue ryegrass straws left in his Mint Juleps. Stone made his own straw using strips of paper and a pencil.

Reference: (https://www.youtube.com/watch?v=-_JhE9lnD6I)

543.

The fastest spinning star discovered is a pulsar named PSR J1748-2446ad and is part of a globular cluster called Terzan 5 in the constellation Sagittarius 18,000 light–years from Earth. It rotates at 24% of the speed of light or 716 times per second at its equator.

Reference: (https://en.wikipedia.org/wiki/PSR_J1748%E2%88%922446ad)

544.

The brand name of norepinephrine, used for septic shock, is Levophed. Many of the older nurses have said that they used to say, "Levophed, leave 'em dead." If patients were sick enough to require norepinephrine to manage their shock, then they were most likely going to die.

Reference: (http://fromnewtoicu.com/blog/2017/1/6/levophed)

545.

Dustin Hoffman's famous "I'm walkin here" scene from "Midnight Cowboy" was completely improvised. As they were filming, a taxi driver cut right through the shot and almost hit Hoffman. In reaction to the taxi, he reacted but stayed in character, giving us the quote we have today.

Reference: (https://www.cbr.com/midnight-cowbody-im-walkin-here/)

546.

Hitler's dog was named Blondi.

Reference: (https://en.wikipedia.org/wiki/Blondi)

547.

One translation of happiness to Chinese is 快乐. The first character means fast or swift, the second character means pleasure.

Reference: (https://www.brighthubeducation.com/learning-chinese/97597-the-three-ways-to-express-happiness-in-chinese/)

548.

The "Rule of Thirds" is a technique used in film and photography that divides the frame into a 3x3 grid, and focuses elements of the frame at the intersecting points on the grid, where our eyes find them most pleasing, and makes the image more comfortable to look at.

Reference: (https://www.shutterstock.com/blog/essential-guide-rule-thirds)

549.

The higher order derivatives of position, after velocity, acceleration, and jerk, are called snap, crackle, and pop.

Reference: (https://en.wikipedia.org/wiki/Pop_(physics))

550.

When 41 members of the Nazi Party were interviewed in 1938 just after Kristallnacht, the Night of Broken Glass, 63% expressed extreme indignation against it, while only 5% expressed approval of racial persecution.

Reference: (https://en.wikipedia.org/wiki/Kristallnacht#Responses_to_Kristallnacht)

551.

Tennessee State Representative Harry Burn was the deciding vote that led to the ratification of the 19th amendment, granting women the right to vote in the U.S. He said: "I know that a mother's advice is always safest for her boy to follow and my mother wanted me to vote for ratification."

Reference: (https://en.wikipedia.org/wiki/Harry_T._Burn)

552.

Male ducks are rapists and female ducks have labyrinth vaginas.

Reference: (https://www.youtube.com/watch?v=Lt4IlxFVT-g&feature=youtu.be)

553.

The largest hailstone ever recorded was the size of a volleyball and weighed 2 pounds.

Reference: (https://www.weather.gov/cae/hail.html)

554.

Foreigner's "Waiting for a Girl Like You" spent a record-setting 10 weeks at number 2 spot on the Billboard charts but never hit number 1, thanks to "Physical" by Olivia Newton John and "I Can't Go for That" by Hall and Oates.

Reference: (https://en.wikipedia.org/wiki/Waiting_for_a_Girl_Like_You)

555.

The Triforce in the Legend Of Zelda series was originally going to be made of electronic chips. The game would have jumped between past and future settings, with the player character acting as the "Link" between them, hence his name.

Reference: (https://mynintendonews.com/2012/11/04/miyamoto-talks-about-the-origin-of-link/)

556.

Uranus contains large amounts of Hydrogen Sulfide, giving it a smell similar to your anus.

Reference: (http://time.com/5252381/uranus-stinks-smell/)

557.

Metals can grow whiskers over time and cause some hairy problems for electronics.

Reference: (https://en.wikipedia.org/wiki/Whisker_(metallurgy))

558.

HMS Encounter and her crew were saved by the Japanese Navy after the Battle of Java Sea in World War II.

Reference: (http://ww2today.com/2nd-march-1942-rescued-from-the-sea-by-the-japanese-navy)

559.

In Quebec, both spouses keep their birth names after marriage and continue to exercise their civil rights under that name, meaning they must use their birth name in contracts, on credit cards, on their driver's licence, and so on. This rule applies even if they were married outside Quebec.

Reference: (https://www.legalline.ca/legal-answers/change-your-name/)

560.

A song named "Lullaby for a Cat" has real unintended psychological effects such as hypnosis on cats.

Reference:(https://www.soompi.com/article/1313377wpp/experts-share-insight-into-why-epik-highs-lullaby-for-a-cat-really-works)

561.

According to a Reader's Digest field experiment, New York City is the most polite major city, followed by Zurich and Toronto. Mumbai ranked last.

Reference: (https://www.readersdigest.ca/health/relationships/how-polite-are-we/)

562.

The creator of the Nickelodeon show "Pelswick" was a real quadriplegic who became a cartoonist to express the experiences of being handicapped.

Reference: (https://en.wikipedia.org/wiki/John_Callahan_(cartoonist))

563.

While he was drafted into the NBA by the New Jersey Nets, Kyle Korver was traded to the Philadelphia 76ers, basically, for a new copier.

Reference: (http://grantland.com/features/kyle-korver-nba-atlanta-hawks/)

564.

The Chernobyl nuclear plant kept operating for 14 years after the explosion at reactor number 4.

Reference:(http://www.world-nuclear.org/information-library/safety-and-security/safety-of-plants/appendices/early-soviet-reactors-and-eu-accession.aspx)

565.

There's a rare mental disorder called "boanthropy," where in sufferers believe they are cows, they are even found in fields with cows, walking on all fours and chewing grass as if they were a true member of the herd.

Reference:(https://www.pharmaceutical-journal.com/opinion/blogs/nebuchadnezzar-and-boanthropy/11123165.blog?firstPass=false)

566.

There's a manga about Jesus and Buddha living as roommates in modern Japan.

Reference: (https://mangadex.org/title/1912/saint-oniisan)

567.

Stirling Colgate attended Los Alamos Boys School when the Manhattan Project took it over for development of A-bombs, later becoming a physicist contributing still classified information for the development of the H-Bomb, at Los Alamos, and was heir to the Colgate Toothpaste Fortune.

Reference: (https://en.wikipedia.org/wiki/Stirling_Colgate#Early_life_and_education)

568.

The Duke of Wellington did not consider his victory over Napoleon at Waterloo to be his greatest victory, instead considering his victory at the Battle of Assaye over Maratha to be a greater achievement.

Reference: (https://en.wikipedia.org/wiki/Battle_of_Assaye)

569.

Due to a perception that prunes relieve constipation, distributors stopped using the word "prune" on packaging labels in favor of "dried plums".

Reference:(https://en.wikipedia.org/wiki/Prune)

570.

According to Deke Slayton, who was responsible for NASA's crew assignments at the time, fellow Mercury 7 astronaut Gus Grisson more than likely would've commanded the first lunar landing mission and been the first man on the moon had he not died 2 and a half years earlier in the Apollo 1 fire.

Reference: (http://users.umiacs.umd.edu/~oard/apollo/poss_moonwalkers.html)

571.

The Oklahoma State Capitol is the only American legislative building with an active oil rig on its grounds.

Reference:(https://oklahoman.com/article/1974476/our-petunia-capitol-is-only-one-with-an-oil-well)

572.

There are only 12 letters in the Hawaiian alphabet: 5 vowels (a, e, i, o, u) and 7 consonants (h, k, l, m, n, p, w).

Reference: (https://en.wikipedia.org/wiki/Hawaiian_alphabet)

573.

Pat Riley, after playing in the NBA for nine years, became a broadcaster for the Los Angeles Lakers. Once Paul Westhead became head coach of the team, he would bring on Riley as an assistant. Pat Riley would go on to be a head coach in the NBA for 24 years and win five championships.

Reference: (https://en.wikipedia.org/wiki/Pat_Riley#Los_Angeles_Lakers)

574.

Flying Jacob is a Swedish casserole that includes chicken, bananas, fried bacon and peanuts.

Reference:(https://thetakeout.com/how-a-banana-chicken-casserole-became-a-beloved-swedish-1798253861)

575.

The Chicago Pile, a nuclear reactor, wasn't given the name as an nod to another great invention as speculated, it was simply a synonym for "heap".

Reference: (https://en.wikipedia.org/wiki/Chicago_Pile-1#Development)

576.

If you take two uncharged conductors and put them close to each other in a vacuum, they will still be slowly drawn to each other and eventually close the distance between them. This is due to an incredibly tiny attractive force known as the Casimir–Polder force.

Reference: (http://www.math.ucr.edu/home/baez/physics/Quantum/casimir.html)

577.

The Sykes–Picot Agreement was a secret pact between the United Kingdom and France. With assent from Russia and Italy, the pact was to defined to split the Ottoman Empire's territory after World War I and maintain their spheres of influence. This pact also created the the countries of Syria and Iraq.

Reference:(https://en.wikipedia.org/wiki/Sykes%E2%80%93Picot_Agreement#Iraq_and_the_Persian_Gulf)

578.

Composer Danny Elfman was in a band called Oingo Boingo and he sang the song "Weird Science" from the movie of the same name.

Reference: (https://en.wikipedia.org/wiki/Weird_Science_(song))

579.

The Hoff Crab is a deep sea crustacean that survives off hydrothermal vents and was nicknamed after David Hasselhoff because of its hairy chest.

Reference: (https://en.wikipedia.org/wiki/Hoff_crab)

580.

"University Challenge," a U.K. game show running since 1962, was based on an American show called "College Bowl," which ended in 1970.

Reference:(https://en.wikipedia.org/wiki/List_of_British_television_series_based_on_American_television_series)

581.

China and India's combined population now is greater than that of the entire world in 1950.

Reference: (https://en.wikipedia.org/wiki/World_population_estimates)

582.

You are more likely to bum a cigarette off of someone if you whisper into their right ear.

Reference:(https://www.ncbi.nlm.nih.gov/pmc/articles/PMC3258574/#R25)

583.

In the 1850s, Canadian Grand Trunk Railway offered reduced rates, free rides and hiding places to fugitive slaves from American South who sought to escape to Canada.

Reference: (https://www.tvo.org/article/why-harriet-tubman-made-st-catharines-her-home)

584.

14 Members of the Da Silva family from Brazil have six fingers on each hand.

Reference: (https://www.youtube.com/watch?v=LlfPIKQmPok)

585.

Sweden has the largest scale model of the Solar System in the world. It is in the scale of 1:20 million and stretches 950 kilometers across the country.

Reference: (https://en.wikipedia.org/w/index.php?title=Sweden_Solar_System)

586.

The hat worn by Indiana Jones was bought from Herbert Johnson in London. The store still exists today and sells the exact same hat, now called the Raiders Rabbit Poet for £365.

Reference: (https://nothingbutnostalgia.com/raiders-of-the-lost-ark-facts/)

587.

The astronauts on the Skylab Space Station staged a rebellion.

Reference:(https://en.wikipedia.org/wiki/Skylab_controversy)

588.

The dispersal of microscopic particles as a result of flushing a toilet is known as a "Toilet Plume."

Reference: (https://en.wikipedia.org/wiki/Toilet_plume)

589.

The majority of the 1,500 people who died in the sinking of the Titanic did not die by drowning, but rather by hypothermia or injury. While many never made it out of the ship, up to 1000 may have jumped to the water during the final moments, with as many as half of them dying upon impact.

Reference: (https://www.encyclopedia-titanica.org/csi-titanic-who-died-how.html)

590.

For the assassination of Archduke Franz Ferdinand of Austria in 1914, there were 6 assassins taking part in the planned attack.

Reference:(https://en.wikipedia.org/wiki/Assassination_of_Archduke_Franz_Ferdinand)

591.

Historians don't agree on whether or not the Huns ever invaded China.

Reference:(https://en.wikipedia.org/wiki/Huns#Relation_to_the_Xiongnu_and_other_peoples_ca lled_Huns)

592.

James McCune Smith, the first African-American doctor, was rejected from all American colleges and had to attend the University of Glasgow in Scotland, where he graduated at the top of his class.

Reference: (https://en.wikipedia.org/wiki/James_McCune_Smith)

593.

July 17, 1972, saw the first two women special agents enter service at the FBI. They were Susan Roley Malone, a former U.S. Marine, and Joanne Pierce, a former nun.

Reference:(https://www.fbi.gov/video-repository/newss-first-women-agents-susan-roley-malone-interview/view)

594.

Prisoners of war from Nazi Germany during World War II in the United States were allowed access to "whites only" areas of the camps.

Reference: (https://timeline.com/nazi-prisoners-war-texas-f4a0794458ea?gi=de12f875a808)

595.

Brian Eno composed the Windows 95 startup sound.

Reference:(https://www.vice.com/es_latam/article/kz79gz/thump-co-brian-eno-windows-95-sonido-microsoft)

596.

Samuel L. Jackson was nominated for Best Actor as well as Best Supporting Actor by the National Society of Film Critics Awards for his portrayal of Jules Winnfield.

Reference:(https://www.nytimes.com/1995/01/04/movies/pulp-fiction-gets-top-prize-from-national-film-critics.html)

597.

Prince Philip was not allowed to invite his three sisters to his wedding to Princess Elizabeth in 1947, because they were all married to German noblemen, and this would have been considered inappropriate in postwar Britain.

Reference:(https://en.wikipedia.org/wiki/Wedding_of_Princess_Elizabeth_and_Philip_Mountbatten#Groom's_family_2)

598.

When President Herbert Hoover was campaigning for his, ultimately unsuccessful, 1932 re-election campaign, he had to deal with one person who tried to assassinate him with dynamite and another person who removed several spikes from the train tracks his train was on.

Reference: (https://en.wikipedia.org/wiki/Herbert_Hoover#1932_re-election_campaign)

599.

George Miller directed the Mad Max franchise as well as Happy Feet.

Reference: (https://en.wikipedia.org/wiki/George_Miller_(director)#Filmography)

600.

Similar to "The Office," 1970s sitcom "Sanford and Son" was based on an earlier British sitcom called "Steptoe and Son" that originally aired in the United Kingdom between 1962 and 1965.

Reference: (https://en.wikipedia.org/wiki/Sanford_and_Son)

601.

Of the 51 million people living in South Korea; approximately half of the country lives in the Seoul metropolitan area.

Reference: (https://en.wikipedia.org/wiki/Seoul_Capital_Area)

602.

In 1828, a painter named Sarah Goodridge painted a miniature portrait of her own breasts and sent it to a man in what is probably one of the earliest cases of someone sending nudes.

Reference: (https://en.wikipedia.org/wiki/Beauty_Revealed)

603.

A Chinese woman gave birth to twins with different fathers. This phenomenon is called superfecundation.

Reference: (https://www.insider.com/woman-has-chinese-twins-different-fathers-2019-3)

604.

An aquarium was goaded into apologizing after "fat-shaming" one of its otters on social media.

Reference: (https://www.boredpanda.com/fat-otter-people-offended-apology-twitter-monterey-bay-aquarium/?utm_source=google&utm_medium=organic&utm_campaign=organic)

605.

There's a man-made cluster of 300 islands off the coast of Dubai that's made in the shape of a world map, and is named after the countries of the world.

Reference: (https://en.wikipedia.org/wiki/The_World_(archipelago))

606.

Mexico City is built in a bowl with no natural escape for water. Floods in 1629 left the city underwater for 4 years.

Reference: (https://99percentinvisible.org/episode/depave-paradise/)

607.

Cricket is the second most popular sport in the world and it is played outside of country clubs.

Reference: (https://www.worldatlas.com/articles/what-are-the-most-popular-sports-in-the-world.html)

608.

The period-after-opening symbol or PAO symbol is a graphic symbol that identifies the useful lifetime of a cosmetic product after its package has been opened for the first time.

Reference: (https://en.wikipedia.org/wiki/Period-after-opening_symbol)

609.

Tupac Shakur and Peter Dinklage worked together as actors, starring in the 1996 movie "Bullet".

Reference: (https://en.wikipedia.org/wiki/Bullet_(1996_film))

610.

A Confederate raiding ship was still attacking Union boats three months after Appomattox.

Reference: (https://www.alaskapublic.org/2015/04/08/long-after-civil-wars-end-rebel-raiders-fought-on-in-bering-sea/)

611.

The same night as the Great Chicago Fire, several other Midwest cities burned and thousands of people lost their lives in Michigan and Wisconsin.

Reference: (https://www.weather.gov/grb/peshtigofire2)

612.

There are three types of tears. Tears caused by emotions are called psychic tears.

Reference: (https://carta.anthropogeny.org/moca/topics/emotional-lacrimation-crying)

613.

"Chlorine smell" in a pool is caused by chlorine reacting with urine to create trichloramines. Chlorine in water is odorless.

Reference: (https://www.youtube.com/watch?v=S32y9aYEzzo)

614.

Arthur Hailey is credited as a writer on every book and movie that the Airplane movies are based on. "Flight In Danger" (M56), "Zero Hour" (M57), "Runway Zero Eight" (B59), "Airport" (B68 and M70) and "Terror in the Sky" (M71).

Reference: (https://en.wikipedia.org/wiki/Arthur_Hailey)

615.

All U.S. Government issued pens are made by a company named Skillcraft that only employs the blind.

Reference: (https://en.wikipedia.org/wiki/Skilcraft)

616.

The winner of "Survivor" once was a soft core porn star and also shot a puppy with a bow and arrow.

Reference: (https://en.wikipedia.org/wiki/Brian_Heidik)

617.

Actor Joaquin Phoenix got into a traffic accident which flipped over his car, but was rescued by a random passerby who first calmly snatched away Phoenix's cigarette lighter right before it lit up the leaking gas tank. The passerby was Werner Herzog.

Reference: (https://www.yahoo.com/entertainment/joaquin-phoenixs-car-crash-savior-werner-herzog-tells-side-story-174841573.html)

618.

Robert Fortune was a Scottish man who infiltrated the Chinese tea industry in the 19th century, eventually smuggling out tea plants and revealing that the Chinese had been dying their tea with hazardous dyes. This effectively ended the Chinese tea industry at the time.

Reference: (https://www.smithsonianmag.com/history/the-great-british-tea-heist-9866709/?c=y&page=4)

619.

The Russians, using an offshore trawler, attempted to jam NASA's communications with the vehicle during the launches of Apollo 8, 9, and 10. This forced NASA to redesign their antennas to combat the interference.

Reference: (https://www.vanityfair.com/hollywood/2018/12/joann-morgan-nasa-apollo-11-interview)

620.

There's a baseball team in Savannah, Georgia called the Savannah Bananas.

Reference: (https://en.wikipedia.org/wiki/Savannah_Bananas)

621.

House track "King of My Castle" by Wamdue Project used footage from Ghost in the Shell in its official music video as the song references Sigmund Freud's theory of the unconscious, which states that, "the ego is not king of its own castle", as it is not free and is controlled by other forces.

Reference: (https://en.wikipedia.org/wiki/King_of_My_Castle)

622.

The misspelling of Beetlejuice as Betelgeuse in the Tim Burton film is a real thing. It's the brightest star in the Orion constellation, and it's pronounced the same way.

Reference: (https://beetlejuice.fandom.com/wiki/Betelgeuse)

623.

The scene in "Fight Club" where Tyler is explaining the cost of a recall when, "A car built by my company crashes and burns with everyone trapped inside" is based on actual leaked memos from GM and Ford.

Reference: (https://www.legalexaminer.com/legal/gm-recall-defective-ignition-switch-saved-company-1/)

624.

The largest cave in the world is Hang Soon Doong and is located in Vietnam. It could contain an entire city with 40-story skyscrapers and it contains a large underground forest that was able to grow and developed thanks to skylights created by the collapse of parts of its vault.

Reference: (http://www.sondoongcave.org/)

625.

David Bowie composed a video game soundtrack and appeared as two different characters in the game.

Reference: (https://www.polygon.com/2016/1/15/10775600/omikron-the-nomad-soul-free-david-bowie)

626.

The comedian Sasha Baron Cohen's cousin helped formulate the theory of mind blindness in autistic children and developed a thought experiment to recognize autistic children called the Sally-Anne test.

Reference: (http://www.educateautism.com/infographics/sally-anne-test.html)

627.

44% of Chilean voters wanted Pinochet to remain in power rather than becoming a democracy.

Reference: (https://en.wikipedia.org/wiki/1988_Chilean_national_plebiscite)

628.

Hitler's personal physician administered cocaine and adrenaline to him via eye drops.

Reference: (https://en.wikipedia.org/wiki/Theodor_Morell#Substances_administered_to_Hitler)

629.

There's a river where you can go surfing in Munich, Germany's English Garden.

Reference: (https://www.youtube.com/watch?v=FJ8j1Mv6MiI)

630.

You have small bones in your body surrounded by connective tissue. Those are in your knees, feet, wrists, hands and your ears. The ones in your ears are among the smallest in your body.

Reference: (https://en.wikipedia.org/wiki/Sesamoid_bone)

631.

Desertification is a prevalent issue in Africa. It's also caused and exacerbated by overcultivation.

Reference: (https://borgenproject.org/what-are-the-causes-of-desertification/)

632.

The deadliest rocket attack during World War II occurred when the Cine Rex cinema in Antwerp, Belgium was hit by a V-2 rocket on December 16, 1944. 567 people were killed and 11 buildings were destroyed by the explosion.

Reference: (https://en.wikipedia.org/wiki/Cine_Rex)

633.

Lin-Manuel Miranda was bullied in high school by battle rapper and underground legend Immortal Technique, but the two have since reconciled and become friends.

Reference: (https://www.xxlmag.com/news/2016/11/immortal-technique-lin-manuel-miranda-bullying-story/)

634.

Sesame Street had their own chain of U.S. retail stores similar to Disney Stores in the 1990s.

Reference: (https://muppet.fandom.com/wiki/Sesame_Street_General_Store)

635.

Chernobyl New Safe Confinement or Chernobyl Dome is the world's largest moveable metal structure over the Chernobyl nuclear power plant's doomed 4th reactor; the gigantic arch soars 108 meters taller than New York's Statue of Liberty.

Reference:
(https://www.worldrecordacademy.com/biggest/largest_movable_metal_structure_Chernobyl_dome_sets_world_record_216366.html)

636.

Half a byte is called a nibble.

Reference:(https://en.wikipedia.org/wiki/Nibble)

637.

The Canadian basketball team the Toronto Raptors uses the slogan "We The North" despite only two members of the roster being Canadian and two NBA teams being more geographically north than the Raptors, Portland and Milwaukee.

Reference: (https://www.nba.com/raptors/roster)

638.

In 1933, the British explorer Frank Smythe attempted to climb Mt. Everest alone. As the time passed, due to isolation, he became so convinced that someone else was accompanying him on his climb that he offered a piece of cake to his invisible climbing partner.

Reference: (https://www.psypost.org/2016/11/social-isolation-brain-begins-act-strange-ways-preserve-sanity-45946)

639.

Humpback whales will create bubble nets to corral their prey together.

Reference: (https://www.youtube.com/watch?v=z00G0RxeSP0&feature=youtu.be)

640.

Often made fun of, the "Duck and Cover" under your desk method for atomic blast survival is based on real research and real survivor stories. Even a thin barrier like a desk can increase chances of survival.

Reference: (https://99percentinvisible.org/episode/atomic-tattoos/)

641.

There is a mythical creature from Scottish mythology called a nuckelavee. It is a sea demon that resembles a man's torso fused to a horse's back, and it has the ability to destroy crops and spread disease with its breath.

Reference: (https://en.wikipedia.org/wiki/Nuckelavee)

642.

Dogs can understand both human words and emotions.

Reference: (https://www.hillspet.com/dog-care/behavior-appearance/do-dogs-understand-human-words-emotions)

643.

The Tin Man from the Wizard of Oz series was once a man named Nick Chopper. A witch cursed his axe causing it to dismember him over time. He then had each bit replaced until he was completely metal. Upon encountering his surviving human head, they argue as to which one is the real Nick.

Reference: (https://en.wikipedia.org/wiki/Tin_Woodman)

644.

The Oxford English Dictionary credits Shakespeare with creating over 2,000 new words in the English language.

Reference:(https://en.wikipedia.org/wiki/Shakespeare%27s_influence)

645.

There was a real cipher that used the Declaration of Independence as its enciphering text in the late 1800s that would supposedly lead to buried treasure. Unfortunately, it was not written on the back of the Declaration in invisible ink but allegedly on papers in a locked box.

Reference:(https://en.wikipedia.org/wiki/Beale_ciphers)

646.

Scientists in Tel Aviv have found that soon after a bee flies past an Evening Primrose, the flower increases the sugar content of its nectar by 30%. Playing bee sounds has a similar effect, but there is no effect on the flower when other vibrations are emitted.

Reference:(https://www.nationalgeographic.com/science/2019/01/flowers-can-hear-bees-and-make-their-nectar-sweeter/)

647.

James Earl Jones had a terrible stutter as a child and was functionally mute for 8 years because of it. A high school teacher helped him end his silence through Jones' love of poetry.

Reference:(https://en.wikipedia.org/wiki/James_Earl_Jones)

648.

The origin of the term "decimation" came from a punishment in the Roman Army where soldiers were split into groups of 10, straws were drawn and whoever drew the short straw was clubbed, stabbed or stoned to death by the remaining 9. The first recorded instance of this is from 478 BC.

Reference:(https://en.wikipedia.org/wiki/Decimation_%28Roman_army%29)

649.

Captain America's list of things to look up in "Winter Soldier" was varied depending on cinematic release location.

Reference:(https://marvelcinematicuniverse.fandom.com/wiki/Captain_America%27s_To-Do_List#Variations)

650.

Until 1971, Memorial Day was always celebrated on May 30.

Reference:(https://en.wikipedia.org/wiki/Memorial_Day)

651.

In social dynamics, a "critical mass" is a sufficient number of adopters of an innovation in a social system so that the rate of adoption becomes self-sustaining and creates further growth.

Reference:(https://en.wikipedia.org/wiki/Critical_mass_%28sociodynamics%29)

652.

Johnny Mathis "Johnny's Greatest Hits" was the first greatest hits album.

Reference:(https://en.wikipedia.org/wiki/Johnny%27s_Greatest_Hits)"

653.

The Centennial Exhibition in 1876 was attended by 5% of the U.S. population and featured new inventions like the telephone, Heinz ketchup, and root beer. Bananas were introduced and sold for what would be $1.75 per banana in today's money.

Reference:(https://philadelphiaencyclopedia.org/archive/centennial/)

654.

Project X-Ray was an experimental U.S. weapon during World War II, in which Mexican free-tailed bats were strapped with timed-incendiary bombs and dropped from planes. The intended target being the paper and wood structures of Japan that the bats would find to roost and eventually set on fire.

Reference: (https://en.wikipedia.org/wiki/Bat_bomb)

655.

The Preakness Stakes horse race was named after a horse called Preakness, who was named after the town it came from, whose name was derived from a Native American term meaning "quail woods".

Reference:(https://en.wikipedia.org/wiki/Preakness,_New_Jersey)

656.

The morningstar spiked club was the favorite weapon of John of Bohemia, a medieval king who was blind.

Reference: (https://en.wikipedia.org/wiki/Morning_star_(weapon))

657.

Throughout history, people have been prejudice against left-handedness.

Reference: (https://en.wikipedia.org/wiki/Handedness#Negative_appeal)

658.

Tetris pieces have an actual name for them and it's called tetrominos.

Reference: (https://en.wikipedia.org/wiki/Tetromino)

659.

There's a minor planet named after Lindsey Stirling.

Reference: (https://en.wikipedia.org/wiki/Meanings_of_minor_planet_names:_242001%E2%80%93243000#516)

660.

Hagoromo Bungu, a Japanese chalk and office supply company is famous among mathematicians for their product, Hagoromo Fulltouch Chalk, referred to as the Rolls-Royce of Chalk.

Reference: (https://en.wikipedia.org/wiki/Hagoromo_Bungus)

661.

Charles Darwin ate every animal he ever discovered. Seeking out "birds and beasts which were unknown to human palate."

Reference: (https://www.npr.org/sections/thesalt/2015/08/12/430075644/dining-like-darwin-when-scientists-swallow-their-subjects)

662.

When light passing through a medium is surpassed by a charged particle going faster than the speed of light in the medium it gives off a glow called Cherenkov Light.

Reference: (https://www.youtube.com/watch?v=O8cHfoHvElY)

663.

Velcro was created after Swiss inventor George de Mestral noticed Burrs stuck to his dogs coat after a walk.

Reference: (https://en.wikipedia.org/wiki/Arctium)

664.

A Marine called customer service when his M107 .50 caliber sniper rifle failed during a gunfight with the Taliban. After several minutes, the weapon was back in service.

Reference:(https://www.range365.com/marines-in-firefight-call-gun-company-customer-service/)

665.

There are Russian dogs that were bred to hunt wolves, their evolutionary ancestor.

Reference: (https://en.wikipedia.org/wiki/Borzoi)

666.

Originally, movie theaters wanted nothing to do with popcorn, because they didn't want popcorn being ground into carpets and rugs. After sound was added to films in 1927, movies became more popular and the humble snack became the norm, so cinemas started selling it in their lobbies.

Reference:(https://www.smithsonianmag.com/arts-culture/why-do-we-eat-popcorn-at-the-movies-475063/)

667.

Met Éireann, the Irish Meteorological Service, supplied the Allies with weather information despite Ireland's neutrality in the Second World War. The decision to go ahead with the D-day landings was made following a favourable weather report from them.

Reference:(https://en.wikipedia.org/wiki/Met_%C3%89ireann)

668.

The world's first motel was opened back in 1925 in San Luis Obispo, California. A two-room bungalow with kitchen and private garage cost $1.25.

Reference:(https://www.smithsonianmag.com/smart-news/worlds-first-motel-was-luxury-establishment-not-dive-180961384/)

669.

Scientists have created a sonic black hole where sound can never escape.

Reference:(https://www.quantamagazine.org/what-sonic-black-holes-say-about-real-ones-20161108/)

670.

President Jimmy Carter left nuclear codes in the pocket of his suit jacket, and sent it to the dry cleaners. They threw it in the bin.

Reference:(https://www.atomicheritage.org/history/nuclear-briefcases)

671.

Human feet produce around half a pint of sweat each day.

Reference:(https://www.podiatrists.org/visitors/foothealth/faqs/general)

672.

Rats can crawl out of your toilet.

Reference:(https://www.nationalgeographic.com/science/phenomena/2015/08/14/yes-rats-can-swim-up-your-toilet-and-it-gets-worse-than-that/)

673.

Bending machines kill over twice as many people as sharks.

Reference:(https://pureoldies941.com/news/25-shocking-things-more-likely-to-kill-you-than-a-shark/)

674.

In 1911, the Mexican Government killed over 300 chinese immigrants in the city of Torreón, Coahuila. The event touched off a diplomatic crisis between China and Mexico. At one point, it was rumored that China had even dispatched a warship to Mexican waters.

Reference:(https://en.wikipedia.org/wiki/Torre%C3%B3n_massacre)

675.

Paro is an AI seal robot created to help calm and soothe dementia and Alzheimer's patients.

Reference:(https://www.youtube.com/watch?v=oJq5PQZHU-I)

676.

A lava-like material called corium is created during a nuclear reactor meltdown, formed of the fuel, fission products, control rods, structural materials, and anything else it can absorb before cooling down.

Reference:(https://en.wikipedia.org/wiki/Corium_(nuclear_reactor)?repost)

677.

The tools and techniques for making gold leaf have remained virtually unchanged for thousands of years: it's still done by people with hammers today.

Reference: (https://en.wikipedia.org/wiki/Goldbeating)

678.

Pure water is an excellent insulator and does not conduct electricity.

Reference:(https://www.usgs.gov/special-topic/water-science-school/science/conductivity-electrical-conductance-and-water)

679.

Korobeiniki is a traditional russian folk song was later used as main theme for tetris.

Reference: (https://en.wikipedia.org/wiki/Korobeiniki)

680.

Axe Body Spray used to be called "Axis" and was almost discontinued before its rebranding.

Reference:(https://www.youtube.com/watch?v=IKMr6poA-As)

681.

Bad smells usually do not carry bacteria and are not capable of spreading disease.

Reference:(https://www.acs.org/content/acs/en/education/resources/highschool/chemmatters/past-issues/2015-2016/april-2016/open-for-discussion--can-smells-harm-you.html)

682.

Quorum Sensing is a method by which cells communicate population density. Some even communicate between species, and even trade genes adapted to an environment to species not adapted, helping them adapt to it as well with the specialized genes it has developed.

Reference:(https://en.wikipedia.org/wiki/Quorum_sensing#Examples)

683.

The first ever NBA Game took place in Toronto, in 1946.

Reference:(https://www.nba.com/history/firstgame_feature.html)

684.

The average age of marriage has been increasing in the U.K., however, marriage rates have fallen. Average age of marriage in 2016: Straight men (age 37.9). Straight women (age 35.5). Gay men (age 40.8). Lesbian women (age 37.4).

Reference:(https://www.ons.gov.uk/peoplepopulationandcommunity/birthsdeathsandmarriages/marriagecohabitationandcivilpartnerships/bulletins/marriagesinenglandandwalesprovisional/2016)

685.

Metropolis, Illinois was declared Hometown of Superman in 1972 after the Illinois State Legislature passed Resolution 572.

Reference:(https://en.wikipedia.org/wiki/Metropolis,_Illinois)

686.

You're banned from bringing mercury on airplanes because of its reactive properties with aluminum.

Reference: (https://www.faa.gov/hazmat/packsafe/)

687.

Building the International Space Station cost more than $150 billion USD and is the most expensive item ever build.

Reference:(https://en.wikipedia.org/wiki/International_Space_Station#cost)

688.

In one of hundreds of his dangerous visits to the Chernobyl disaster site, nuclear inspector Artur Korneyev was able to take a photo of himself in 1996 near the Elephant Foot, a radioactive mass that initially gave off more than 10,000 roentgens per hour.

Reference:(https://www.atlasobscura.com/articles/the-famous-photo-of-chernobyls-most-dangerous-radioactive-material-was-a-selfie)

689.

Botox is the most poisonous substance known to man. A couple of teaspoons are enough to kill everyone in the U.K.

Reference:(https://www.bbc.co.uk/news/magazine-24551945)

690.

Some Capuchin Monkeys attend Monkey College to learn how to help disabled people with everyday tasks.

Reference:(http://time.com/longform/service-monkeys-quadriplegia/)

691.

Muscles make grumbling sounds.

Reference:(http://res.marcodonnarumma.com/blog/how-human-muscles-sound/)

692.

In 1942, Japanese troops landed and occupied the Aleutian Islands of Attu and Kiska. They were driven out entirely a year later between May and August, 1943, by U.S. and Canadian forces. This was the first significant foreign occupation of American soil since the War of 1812.

Reference:(https://en.wikipedia.org/wiki/Invasion_of_the_United_States#Imperial_Japan)

693.

The character Arnold of "Hey Arnold!" originally appeared in a series of claymation shorts on "Sesame Street."

Reference:(https://www.youtube.com/watch?v=uBlzuEQiRfU&feature=youtu.be)

694.

There's a temple in India dedicated to rats. The temple has about 20,000 rats in it, and you need to take your shoes off to enter. People believe the rats are a form of the goddess. Many people make offerings to the rats; some even eat and sleep with them.

Reference:(https://www.vice.com/sv/article/9bkvj7/karni-mata-deshnoke-india-rat-temple)

695.

When London Underground's first escalators were installed in 1911 a one-legged man - William "Bumper" Harris - was employed to ride the escalators and demonstrate to a sceptical public the safety of the new machines. Ironically, he had lost his leg in an earlier underground accident.

Reference:(https://www.timeout.com/london/blog/25-things-you-didnt-know-about-the-tube-051616)

696.

Chairs, sofas and sofa beds sent 669,992 U.S. residents to the emergency room in 2017 and 51,319 sought emergency care because of injuries related to sound recording equipment.

Reference:(https://www.cpsc.gov/s3fs-public/2017-Neiss-data-highlights.pdf?3i3POG9cN.rIyu2ggrsUkD1XU_zoiFRP)

697.

No VAT is charged in plain biscuits or cakes in the U.K.

Reference:(https://www.icaew.com/archive/about-icaew/news/press-release-archive/2016-press-releases/jaffa-cake-is-it-a-cake-or-a-biscuit-vats-the-difference)

698.

The boundary between the Earth's atmosphere and outer space is called the Kármán Line.

Reference:(https://en.wikipedia.org/wiki/K%C3%A1rm%C3%A1n_line)

699.

People change light bulbs in tall places with light bulb changing poles instead of ladders.

Reference:(https://www.youtube.com/watch?v=36x37YIKjcQ&feature=youtu.be)

700.

The international date line isn't straight. It actually curves around Alaska to keep all of Alaska as having the same date. It also keeps Russia and Alaska as having different dates.

Reference:(https://en.wikipedia.org/wiki/International_Date_Line#Geography)

701.

In the collection of the National Museum of Scotland in Edinburgh is an unusual artefact; a block of limestone, roughly hewn and damaged in places, and weighing around half a metric ton. This stone is a "casing stone" from Egypt. Circa 2,600 B.C. it was on the Great Pyramid of Khufu in Giza.

Reference:(http://www.egyptian-architecture.com/JAEA1/JAEA1_Lightbody)

702.

The inventor of the USB had originally intended for it to be flippable, however, that idea was scrapped due to the extra cost. Despite USB becoming the standard, he still regrets that decision. "In hindsight, we blew it," he said.

Reference:(https://www.pcworld.com/article/2999836/happy-birthday-usb-the-standard-turns-20-and-proud-inventor-ajay-bhatt-tells-all.html)

703.

Pigeons are a invasive non-native feral animals. They are the world's oldest domestic bird and were domesticated between 5,000 and 10,000 years ago from the Rock Dove. The birds adapted well to life in the city because building ledges mimic sea cliffs where they originally lived and nested.

Reference:(https://www.cell.com/current-biology/fulltext/S0960-9822(11)01458-8?_returnURL=https%3A%2F%2Flinkinghub.elsevier.com%2Fretrieve%2Fpii%2FS0960982211014588%3Fshowall%3Dtrue)

704.

To promote the 1992 film "Son In Law," a competition was held to marry Pauly Shore. The winner also received a bumblebee ring and a yo-yo that lights up.

Reference:(https://ew.com/article/1993/07/30/entertainment-news-july-30-1993/)

705.

Hurricanes, typhoons and cyclones are the same kind of storm, each name corresponding to a geographic location.

Reference:(https://www.redcross.org/get-help/how-to-prepare-for-emergencies/types-of-emergencies/hurricane/hurricane-vs-typhoon.html)

706.

The use of phallometric evidence in Canadian criminal courts has steadily increased since the early 1980s.

Reference:(http://jaapl.org/content/43/2/141)

707.

Operation Copperhead occurred when the British used a double of general Montgomery to fool the Germans into thinking that the allies were going to invade the south of France.

Reference:(https://en.wikipedia.org/wiki/Operation_Copperhead)

708.

In 1909, the United States Government confiscated Coca-Cola products because the high caffeine content breached a food safety law. This case went all to the way to the Supreme Court, and the government won, forcing Coca-Cola to pay all court costs and reduce their product's caffeine content.

Reference:(https://www.apa.org/monitor/2009/02/coca-cola)

709.

The female given name Evolet originated from critically panned movie "10,000 BC."

Reference:(https://en.wikipedia.org/wiki/10,000_BC_(film))

710.

During World War II, King George VI was at war with Germany as the King of the U.K., but as King of Ireland he was also at peace with Germany and validated the credentials of German ambassadors. After World War II, he was at war with himself as King of India and separately as King of Pakistan.

Reference:(https://en.wikipedia.org/wiki/Commonwealth_realm#cite_note-War-36)

711.

The moving visual sensations of stars and patterns we see when we close our eyes is called Phosphenes.

Reference:(https://www.huffpost.com/entry/why-do-i-see-patterns-when-i-close-my-eyes_b_7597438)

712.

Early spy satellites dropped their film canisters from space which were subsequently caught in mid-air by military airplanes.

Reference:(https://www.youtube.com/watch?v=uy0p5ZoCr80&feature=youtu.be)

713.

The act of scaling defensive walls or ramparts with the aid of ladders, a prominent and dangerous siege warfare tactic in medieval times, is called "Escalade".

Reference: (https://en.wikipedia.org/wiki/Escalade)

714.

The Chirihama Nagisa Driveway, in Ishikawa Prefecture, Japan, is an 8 kilometer long section of road that's actually a beach.

Reference:(https://www.visitkanazawa.net/chirihama-nagisa-driveway)

715.

In Sweden, if you want to sell your old IKEA furniture on the Swedish equivalent to Craigslist, called Blocket, IKEA will pay for your ad.

Reference:(https://ww8.ikea.com/se/sv/ext/ikea-family/blocket/)

716.

Miss Scarlet, in the 1972 edition of the Parker Brothers classic board game "Clue", was portrayed by Kedakai Turner, wife of Inside the Actors Studio host James Lipton.

Reference:(https://boardgamegeek.com/image/541034/clue)

717.

Finland has 178,947 islands.

Reference:(https://en.wikipedia.org/wiki/List_of_islands_of_Finland)

718.

Rabies is not 100% fatal once you've reached critical stage.

Reference:(https://www.nature.com/scitable/blog/viruses101/is_rabies_really_100_fatal)

719.

The Imp of the Perverse is a metaphor for the urge to do exactly the wrong thing in a given situation for the sole reason that it is possible for wrong to be done. The impulse is compared to an imp, a small demon, which leads an otherwise decent person into mischief.

Reference:(https://en.wikipedia.org/wiki/The_Imp_of_the_Perverse)

720.

Exposure to particles from burning candles causes greater damage than the same dose of diesel exhaust fumes. Effects included lung inflammation and toxicity, arteriosclerosis, and ageing effects on chromosomes in the lungs and spleen.

Reference:(https://www.theguardian.com/world/2018/dec/14/beware-of-burning-candles-when-enjoying-hygge-say-scientists)

721.

The first recorded and scientifically named dinosaur bone was named "Scrotum humanum". Belonging to a Megalosaurus, it was also known as the Predatory Scrotum.

Reference:(https://io9.gizmodo.com/the-first-scientific-name-ever-given-to-a-dinosaur-foss-5955550)

722.

Mexico City's Tepito barrio has a high crime rate but most residents who live there do not want to leave. Tepito has its own rules and most outside authorities abide by them as it is a rich source of bribe money

Reference: (https://en.wikipedia.org/wiki/TepitoI)

723.

In 1903, the New York Times declared that "flying machines" were essentially a waste of time—only a week before the Wright brothers successfully flew their airplane at Kitty Hawk, North Carolina.

Reference:(https://www.nytimes.com/1903/10/09/archives/flying-machines-which-do-not-fly.html)

724.

The Wood Frogs have adapted to cold climates by freezing over the winter. During this time, they stop breathing and their hearts stop beating. Their bodies produce a special antifreeze substance that prevents ice from freezing within their cells.

Reference:(https://www.nwf.org/Educational-Resources/Wildlife-Guide/Amphibians/Wood-Frog)

725.

There has been a case where coconut water has been used as replacement for IV fluid for 2 days, infusing about 2 and half litres of coconut water. The patient recovered and was discharged after 3 days.

Reference:(https://www.abc.net.au/science/articles/2014/12/09/4143229.htm)

726.

3 of the first 4 U.S. Presidents died on July 4th.

Reference:(https://en.wikipedia.org/wiki/List_of_Presidents_of_the_United_States_by_date_of_death)

727.

During his time as a prisoner of war, Alexis Casdagli made numerous cross-stitches. One of them was so good that the Germans displayed them in his POW camp for everyone to see, unaware of a secret message stitched into his handiwork. The message, in Morse code, reads "God save the King" and "Fuck Hitler".

Reference:(https://www.telegraph.co.uk/news/9009004/British-prisoner-of-War-stitched-hidden-anti-Hitler-message-into-Nazi-quilt.html)

728.

The only casualty of the infamous Tacoma Narrows Bridge collapse of 1940 was a cocker spaniel named Tubby, who refused to leave the car he was in and bit one of the people attempting to rescue him. His body was never found.

Reference:(https://en.wikipedia.org/wiki/Tacoma_Narrows_Bridge_(1940))

729.

Disney World has a Mickey-shaped solar farm big enough to power 2 of its parks.

Reference:(https://wdwnt.com/2018/10/new-solar-power-facility-at-walt-disney-world-to-open-before-end-of-2018/)

730.

The U.S. Vice President's Oath of Office includes the line, "I take this obligation freely, without any mental reservation or purpose of evasion...", which is omitted from the much shorter Presidential Oath.

Reference:(https://bensguide.gpo.gov/j-oath-office?highlight=WyJjb25zdGl0dXRpb24iLCJjb25zdGl0dXRpb24ncyJd)

731.

Even with modern medicine, one in four pregnancies end up as a miscarriage.

Reference:(https://www.tommys.org/pregnancy-information/im-pregnant/early-pregnancy/how-common-miscarriage)

732.

Even before the surgeon general issued his report on the dangers of tobacco, Mad Magazine went on an anti-smoking crusade ridiculing big tobacco, as agencies, and even smokers. Also, before it became law, Mad Magazine's offices were smoke free and none of their content featured smoking.

Reference:(https://www.newyorker.com/culture/culture-desk/mad-magazines-glorious-anti-smoking-campaign)

733.

Les Paul was one of the pioneers of multitrack music recording.

Reference:(https://en.wikipedia.org/wiki/History_of_multitrack_recording)

734.

The first person to be tried and hung for treason in the United States was a citizen who was angry at the placement of an American flag in formally Confederate North Carolina and tore it down. He was publicly hung in front of the mint building he took it down from.

Reference:(https://en.wikipedia.org/wiki/William_Bruce_Mumford)

735.

June Carter and Merle Kilgore originally wrote "Ring of Fire", which was about June's volatile relationship with Johnny Cash.

Reference:(https://en.wikipedia.org/wiki/Ring_of_Fire_(song))

736.

In 1989, the U.S. government passed a bill called the "Whistleblower Protection Plan" that protects any federal employee that reports: suspicious activity, gross waste of funds, regulations, danger to public health, violation of laws,....etc; Against any agency who decides to retaliate.

Reference: (https://www.whistleblowers.gov/)

737.

"London Broil" is a North American culinary method of cooking certain cuts of beef, which have no traditional basis in the U.K. There's nothing "London" about a London Broil.

Reference:(https://en.wikipedia.org/wiki/London_broil)

738.

Devils Heads are strange gray objects, each about an inch or two across with four curved spike-like horns. They are the fruit of European water chestnut, an invasive aquatic plant released inadvertently into waters of the Northeast United States in the late 1800s.

Reference:(https://www.njpalisades.org/devilsHeads.html)

739.

The terms First World, Second World and Third World countries were introduced during the Cold War. Third World countries simply meant the countries which didn't align with either NATO and capitalism (First World) or communism and the Soviet Union (Second World).

Reference:(https://borgenproject.org/definition-of-a-third-world-country/)

740.

Oprah Gail Winfrey was born Orpah, after a character in the Bible, but people mispronounced it regularly and the name "Oprah" stuck.

Reference: (https://en.wikipedia.org/wiki/Oprah_Winfrey#Early_life)

741.

A giraffes tongue is a half meter long.

Reference:(https://giraffeconservation.org/facts/how-long-is-a-giraffes-tongue-what-colour-is-it/)

742.

Before the advent of anesthesia, general surgeons dreaded performing surgeries, and it was uncommon for patients to talk about their procedures as it could reawaken, "suppressed memories of a necessary torture."

Reference:(https://theconversation-com.cdn.ampproject.org/v/s/theconversation.com/amp/a-short-history-of-anaesthesia-from-unspeakable-agony-to-unlocking-consciousness-74748?amp_js_v=0.1#referrer=https%3A%2F%2Fwww.google.com&amp_tf=From%20%251%24s&ampshare=https%3A%2F%2Ftheconversation.com%2Fa-short-history-of-anaesthesia-from-unspeakable-agony-to-unlocking-consciousness-74748)

743.

In the 18th and 19th centuries, pills made out of the metal antimony would be taken as a laxative but not dissolve, so they'd be rescued, reused, and even passed down as heirlooms.

Reference: (https://en.wikipedia.org/wiki/Antimony_pill)

744.

Earth is long overdue for a reversal of its magnetic poles. Earth's magnetic field protects us from cosmic rays so a reversal could cause catastrophic events such as rendering entire regions uninhabitable and causing cell phones to not work.

Reference: (https://futurism.com/earths-magnetic-poles-overdue-switch)

745.

Maj. Charles Carpenter, "Bazooka Charlie", strapped bazookas to his light artillery spotting airplane and attacked German tanks in World War II.

Reference:(https://tacairnet.com/2015/10/01/bazooka-charlie-and-his-nazi-tank-killin-grasshopper/)

746.

The first man in England to use an umbrella in the early 1750s, Jonas Hanway, was pelted with insults and trash as men using umbrellas was taboo. In the minds of many Brits, umbrella usage was symptomatic of a weakness of character. The British also regarded umbrellas as too French.

Reference:(https://www.atlasobscura.com/articles/the-public-shaming-of-englands-first-umbrella-user)

747.

In the iconic photo with Sean Connery in "From Russia with Love", James Bond is brandishing a Walther LP53, a pellet gun.

Reference: (https://www.jamesbondlifestyle.com/product/walther-lp53)

748.

Social network Bebo was bought by AOL for US$850 million. 5 years later, the original owners bought it back for US$1 million.

Reference: (https://en.wikipedia.org/wiki/Bebo?AOL#History)

749.

Kim Phuc Phan Thi, the then-little-girl from the infamous Napalm photo, received Germany's international peace prize, Dresden Peace Prize, on February 11, 2019.

Reference: (http://time.com/5527355/napalm-girl-kim-phuc-phan-thi-dresden-prize/)

750.

During the Battle of the Bulge, General McAulliffe responded to the German's surrender demands with "Nuts!" in English, which was then translated, with the help of Bud Harper, to "Go to hell!" in German.

Reference: (https://www.army.mil/article/92856/the_story_of_the_nuts_reply)

751.

DJ Wika, an 80 year old woman from Warsaw, Poland, took up mixing at the young age of 60, while a manager at a senior club, and hasn't stopped since.

Reference: (https://www.youtube.com/watch?v=72PRW_pJRoE&feature=youtu.be)

752.

The United States has 7 uniformed services, including the Public Health Service Commissioned Corps, whose officers wear the same uniforms as the Navy and who serve under the Surgeon General.

Reference:(https://en.wikipedia.org/wiki/United_States_Public_Health_Service_Commissioned_Corps)

753.

Comedian Conan O'Brien, host of the U.S. talk show "Conan," is a Harvard graduate and is on the board of directors for the John F. Kennedy Presidential Library and Museum.

Reference: (https://www.jfklibrary.org/about-us/jfk-library-foundation/board-of-directors)

754.

The newspaper of Jefferson, Texas is called the Jefferson Jimplecute.

Reference: (https://en.wikipedia.org/wiki/Jefferson_Jimplecute)

755.

Canada is the world's leading supplier of National Hockey League players. 43% of all 2018 to 2019 season NHL players were born in Canada.

Reference:(https://thehockeynews.com/news/article/where-in-the-world-do-nhl-players-come-from)

756.

Your body emits different chemicals in your tears depending on why you're crying. When you cry for an emotional reason, watching a sad movie, or due to physical pain those emotional tears contain leucine-enkephalin, an endorphin that reduces pain and works to improve mood.

Reference: (https://science.howstuffworks.com/life/inside-the-mind/emotions/crying1.htm)

757.

France has the world's largest Exclusive Economic Zone.

Reference:(https://www.worldatlas.com/articles/countries-with-the-largest-exclusive-economic-zones.html)

758.

Neil Young actually performed the song "Sweet Home Alabama" at a concert in 1977.

Reference: (http://www.sugarmtn.org/song.php?song=21)

759.

The top 10% of drinkers account for more than half of all alcohol consumed in the U.S. Which equates to them consuming an average 73.85 drinks per week.

Reference:(https://www.inc.com/jeff-haden/the-top-10-percent-drink-way-more-than-you-think.htmls)

760.

Kimbo Slice, real name Kevin Ferguson, had 6 children. Their names were Kevin Ferguson Jr, Kevin Ferguson II, Kevlar Ferguson, Kassandra Ferguson, Kiara Ferguson and Kevina Ferguson.

Reference: (https://en.wikipedia.org/wiki/Kimbo_Slice)

761.

The "Titanic" movie caused a craze in Afghanistan that the Taliban had to ban the DiCaprio hairstyle that young boys were wearing,

Reference:(https://www.news24.com/xArchive/Archive/Titanic-craze-grips-Afghan-capital-20001116)

762.

Large lobsters are 70 years old. A lobster that weighs 3 pounds is an estimated 15 to 20 years old, and a 25 pound lobster would be approximately 75 to 100 years old.

Reference: (https://www.bayleys.com/seafood-and-lobster-facts/)

763.

There is a Gecko nicknamed "The Fuck You Lizard" for the sound it makes at night.

Reference: (https://www.youtube.com/watch?v=Z1N2ACztZMI&feature=youtu.be)

764.

People living at higher elevations have a higher rate of suicide. The correlation between elevation and suicide risk was present even when the researchers control for known suicide risk factors, including age, gender, race, and income. The cause for the increased risk is as yet unknown.

Reference:(https://en.wikipedia.org/wiki/Effects_of_high_altitude_on_humans#Long-term_effects)

765.

All those images and stories of the Black Plague in history and modern times talking about and showing people breaking out in sores all over their bodies were incorrect.

Reference:(https://www.npr.org/sections/goatsandsoda/2017/08/18/542435991/those-iconic-images-of-the-plague-thats-not-the-plague)

766.

The USS Constitution, currently docked in Boston, only has 8% to 10% of the original wood of the ship launched in 1797.

Reference:(https://ussconstitutionmuseum.org/2018/04/13/rebuilt-preserved-restored-uss-constitution-across-the-centuries/)

767.

In most elevators in the U.S., at least in any built or installed since the early nineties, the door-close button doesn't work. It is there mainly to make you think it works. It does work if, say, a fireman needs to take control, but you need a key, and a fire, to do that.

Reference:(https://www.newyorker.com/magazine/2008/04/21/up-and-then-down?fbclid=IwAR3kyPBo2j9XvWVpleV9UWsafsdhhZ8vE9K_FkKGSzHyzjQLXXONxEm-xdg)

768.

Alan Thicke composed the theme for a version of "Wheel of Fortune."

Reference:(https://en.wikipedia.org/wiki/Wheel_of_Fortune_%28U.S._game_show%29?wprov=sfla1)

769.

The phrase "long time no see" likely originated as a humorous interpretation of a Native American greeting.

Reference: (https://blog.oxforddictionaries.com/2015/06/18/9-words-with-offensive-origins/)

770.

The only difference between hair and fur is density, otherwise they are chemically the same.

Reference: (https://www.scientificamerican.com/article/what-is-the-difference-be/?redirect=1)

771.

In 1951, a little known German company called Adidas purchased a 3-stripe brand logo from a small Finnish company called Karhu for the equivalent of €1,600 and two bottles of "good whiskey". The 3-stripes have gone on to become one of the most recognizable logos in history.

Reference: (https://karhu.com/blog/three-stripes-trademark-sold-to-adidas/)

772.

Jefferson Airplanes' two best known songs were re-recordings of minor hits by Grace Slick's first band.

Reference: (https://en.wikipedia.org/wiki/The_Great_Society_(band))

773.

Ricky Martin has a foundation to help stop human trafficking. He helped rescue three girls from being sold into slavery, which led to him creating the foundation.

Reference: (http://rickymartinfoundation.org/about/)

774.

At 83 years old, Michael Caine changed his legal name because He stated, "An airport security guard would say, 'Hi, Michael Caine,' and suddenly I'd give him a passport with a different name on it. I could stand there for an hour. So I changed my name."

Reference: (http://time.com/4418838/michael-caine-maurice-micklewhite-name-change/)

775.

Aurochs, the prehistoric ancestors of modern-day domesticated cattle, was roughly twice the size of modern bovine. According to Julius Caesar, Germanic tribes in northern Europe hunted these beasts and collected their horns for sport and status.

Reference: (http://penelope.uchicago.edu/Thayer/E/Roman/Texts/Caesar/Gallic_War/6C*.html)

776.

Ancient Egyptians made statues out of otters.

Reference: (https://www.metmuseum.org/art/collection/search/544088)

777.

Woolly Mammoths were still alive by the time the pyramids at Giza were completed. The last woolly mammoths died out on Wrangel Island, north of Russia, only 4,000 years ago, leaving several centuries where the pyramids and mammoths existed at the same time.

Reference:(https://www.bbc.co.uk/programmes/articles/1XkbKQwt49MpxWpsJ2zpfQk/13-mammoth-facts-about-mammoths)

778.

Alfred Hitchcock was on an FBI watch list for researching the atomic bomb for his film "Notorious" a year before Hiroshima.

Reference:(http://hometown-pasadena.com/history/when-a-master-of-suspense-met-a-caltech-scientist/30914)

779.

When John Pemberton first brought Coca Cola on the market, on May 29th in 1886, it was a lucky result of his search for a morphine-free painkiller. He sold the Coca Cola rights soon after, to pay for his expensive morphine addiction.

Reference:(https://www.pharmacytimes.com/careers-news/5-facts-about-famous-pharmacist-john-pemberton-coca-cola-inventor)

780.

The mask worn by Michael Myers in the "Halloween" film franchise was actually a Captain Kirk mask painted white.

Reference:(https://www.startrek.com/article/was-michael-myers-halloween-mask-william-shatners-face)

781.

South Italy is known as "noon".

Reference: (https://en.wikipedia.org/wiki/Southcrn_Italy?wprov=sfti1)

782.

Some LEDs can output more energy as light than the amount of electrical energy going into them, by taking thermal energy from their environment.

Reference: (https://journals.aps.org/prl/abstract/10.1103/PhysRevLett.108.097403)

783.

Tolkien never once describes the elves as having pointed ears.

Reference: (https://middle-earth.xenite.org/do-tolkiens-elves-have-pointy-ears/)

784.

Russia gave the United States a memorial to the victims of the September 11th Terror Attacks.

Reference: (https://en.wikipedia.org/wiki/To_the_Struggle_Against_World_Terrorism)

785.

Cameron Lacroix is an American computer hacker best known for the hacking of Paris Hilton's cellular phone, accessing LexisNexis, and defacing Burger King's twitter account. It's estimated that he's caused about $1 million in damages.

Reference: (https://en.wikipedia.org/wiki/Cameron_Lacroix)

786.

In the 1930s, after Frank Schutt, General Manager of The Peabody hotel in Memphis, returned from a hunting trip he thought it would be funny to place some of his live duck decoys in the Peabody fountain. Thus began a Peabody tradition which was to become internationally famous.

Reference: (https://www.peabodymemphis.com/ducks-en.html)

787.

The paint company Dulux hired and paid a research scientist to actually watch paint dry. His full time job involves carefully observing the changing colors and particles of paint as it dries – both on walls as well as under a microscope.

Reference:(https://www.odditycentral.com/news/guy-actually-gets-paid-to-watch-paint-dry.html)

788.

Three on a match is a superstition among soldiers. When the first soldier lit his cigarette, the enemy would see the light. When the second soldier lit his cigarette, the enemy would take aim and when the third soldier lit his cigarette, the enemy would fire and that soldier would be shot.

Reference: (https://en.wikipedia.org/wiki/Three_on_a_match_(superstition))

789.

In English speaking countries outside of North America, the noun "curb" is spelled "kerb".

Reference: (https://grammarist.com/spelling/curb-kerb/)

790.

In 1986, General Motors launched a reorganisation plan that was so expensive, $35 billion, that they could have bought both Toyota and Nissan with the money. Ultimately the aforementioned purchase of Japanese automakers would have earned GM more in dividends.

Reference: (https://en.wikipedia.org/wiki/Roger_Smith_(executive)#Drive_for_modernization)

791.

The National Park Service uses 75 millimeter anti-tank cannons from World War II to trigger controlled avalanches.

Reference: (https://military.wikia.org/wiki/M20_recoilless_rifle)

792.

Wheel of Fortune used to have prizes on the show that the winning contestant could spend their winnings on.

Reference:(https://www.metv.com/stories/who-remembers-when-wheel-of-fortune-had-shopping)

793.

Dopamine itself is actually a neurotoxin. It will shut down cellular respiration and kill neurons that are actively producing it.

Reference: (https://en.wikipedia.org/wiki/Neurotoxin#Dopamine)

794.

When the Lyon's Inn, an Inn of Chancery, was dissolved on 1863, it was run by only two Ancients, neither of whom had any idea what their duties were, and the Inn had not dined for over a century.

Reference: (https://en.wikipedia.org/wiki/Lyon%27s_Inn)

795.

Bose, the audio equipment company, was founded by Amar Bose, an MIT engineering professor who bought a high-end stereo speaker system in 1956 and was disappointed of its sound quality. Despite owning Bose, he remained a professor. He donated most of Bose shares to MIT as non-voting.

Reference: (https://en.wikipedia.org/wiki/Amar_Bose)

796.

The phone number featured in Soulja Boy's 2008 song ''Kiss Me thru the Phone'' would connect to an unsuspecting family in Manchester, England. They were inundated with calls after fans dialled the number but mistyped the international dialing code prefix.

Reference: (https://en.wikipedia.org/wiki/Kiss_Me_thru_the_Phone)

797.

Andy Kaufman got so tired of doing his "Foreign Man" character for the portrayal of Latka Gravas in "Taxi" that in order to appease him, the writers wrote in that Gravas had multiple personality disorder so he could do other characters on the show.

Reference: (https://en.wikipedia.org/wiki/Taxi_(TV_series))

798.

Before he made it as a cartoonist with "The Far Side", Gary Larson was an animal cruelty investigator with the Seattle Humane Society. While driving to the interview for the job, he accidentally hit a dog.

Reference: (https://www.sun-sentinel.com/news/fl-xpm-1987-08-23-8703090658-story.html)

799.

If a cow eats the white snakeroot plant, its milk becomes poisonous. The "milk sickness" that comes from drinking it killed thousands of people in the 19th century U.S.

Reference: (https://en.wikipedia.org/wiki/Milk_sickness)

800.

To free yourself from wet quicksand, just to release one foot, you would need a force equivalent of the strength to lift a medium-sized car. Sinking isn't what kills you, but being stuck and the incoming high tide.

Reference:(http://www.bbc.com/future/story/20160323-can-quicksand-really-suck-you-to-your-death)

801.

A man wrestled a bull shark to retrieve his nephew's severed arm; surgeons were able to successfully re-attach the arm.

Reference:(http://edition.cnn.com/2001/CAREER/trends/07/26/shark.attack.surgeons.focus/index.html)

802.

In 2014, an 89 year old World War II veteran, Bernard Shaw went missing from his nursing home. It turned out that he went to Normandy for the 70th anniversary of D-Day landings against the nursing home's orders. He left the home wearing a grey mack concealing the war medals on his jacket.

Reference:(https://www.itv.com/news/update/2014-06-06/d-day-veteran-pulls-off-nursing-home-escape/)

803.

Princess Diana's late boyfriend Dodi Al-Fayed, who was also in the fatal car crash in 1997, was first cousins with Jamal Khashoggi.

Reference: (https://en.wikipedia.org/wiki/Jamal_Khashoggi)

804.

The slang term "shorty" or "shawty" was first used and popularized by the Three Stooges in the late 1930s.

Reference: (https://en.wikipedia.org/wiki/Shawty_(slang))

805.

In 1925, there was a project called "Plan Voisin" by renowned architect Le Corbusier to destroy the historical center of Paris and replace it with concrete mega towers that could host up to 3 million people.

Reference: (https://www.businessinsider.com/le-corbusiers-plan-voisin-for-paris-2013-7)

806.

Scientists can determine which ancient animals and plants existed in an area by extracting DNA from as little as 2 grams of sediment.

Reference: (https://www.youtube.com/watch?v=_9Kd_Bvn7o4)

807.

An 98 year old woman received a Congressional Gold Medal decades after her service as a spy in World War II.

Reference:(https://www.msn.com/en-us/news/good-news/decades-after-her-secretive-service-wwii-spy-honored-with-congressional-medal/ar-AAC2JvR?ocid=ientp)

808.

"Panda Pornography" are movies depicting mating pandas shown to captive pandas who are unenthusiastic about breeding.

Reference: (https://en.wikipedia.org/wiki/Panda_pornography)

809.

The male platypus is venomous. It has a crooked spur on the heel of each rear foot which can inject venom that is resistant to conventional painkillers.

Reference:(https://slate.com/technology/2015/06/platypus-venom-painful-immediate-long-lasting-impervious-to-painkillers.html)

810.

In 1986, the city of Cleveland released 1.5 million balloons in the air in order to break a Guinness World Record. The event was never recognized by Guinness.

Reference: (https://www.youtube.com/watch?v=n0CT8zrw6lw)

811.

On average, cats spend two thirds of every day sleeping. That means that a nine-year-old cat has been awake for only three years of its life.

Reference: (https://www.meowingtons.ca/blogs/news/10-interesting-cat-facts)

812.

NASA put a penny on Mars to calibrate the cameras on the rover Curiosity.

Reference: (https://photojournal.jpl.nasa.gov/catalog/PIA16131)

813.

A finger is technically a limb.

Reference: (https://en.wikipedia.org/wiki/Finger)

814.

There is a neighborhood in Davis, California where all the streets are named after characters and locations from "Lord of the Rings" and "The Hobbit."

Reference: (https://www.sacbee.com/news/business/real-estate-news/article168283157.html)

815.

Dennis Farina, who played Det. Joe Fontana on "Law and Order," was actually a cop with the Chicago Police Department burglary division.

Reference:(https://www.latimes.com/entertainment/movies/la-xpm-2013-jul-22-la-et-mn-dennis-farina-dead-cop-turned-actor-20130722-story.html)

816.

Before he was an actor, Mr. T was a sought after bodyguard, charging as much as $10,000 a day for his services.

Reference: (https://en.wikipedia.org/wiki/Mr._T???)

817.

Funai Electric Co. of Japan was the last known company in the world to manufacture VHS equipment, which ceased production in 2016.

Reference: (https://en.wikipedia.org/wiki/Funai#VHS_videotape)

818.

The common foot, as in measurement, used in ancient Greece in the construction of the Parthenon is virtually the same as the current Imperial foot.

Reference: (https://www.youtube.com/watch?v=MLCW0zKR4xk&feature=youtu.be)

819.

There are at least eight other international versions of "The Office" besides those from the U.K. and the U.S., including series produced in Germany, France, Israel, Chile and Sweden.

Reference: (https://en.wikipedia.org/wiki/The_Office#Counterparts)

820.

Halle Berry hated the movie "Catwoman" so much that she showed up in person to accept her Razzie award. In her acceptance speech she said "I want to thank Warner Brothers. Thank you for putting me in a piece of shit god-awful movie."

Reference: (https://www.youtube.com/watch?v=U-7s_yeQuDg)

821.

US 442nd Infantry Regiment, comprised of Japanese Americans, were awarded 18,000 medals in 2 years.

Reference: (https://en.wikipedia.org/wiki/442nd_Infantry_Regiment_(United_States))

822.

Doctors managed to keep Hisashi Ouchi alive for 83 days after he was blasted with 17 sieverts of radiation, the highest recorded dose any human has ever received. Estimated to be the equivalent to the epicenter of the Hiroshima bomb, the radiation annihilated his DNA and immune system.

Reference:(https://icantbelieveitsnonfiction.com/2018/02/14/hisashi-ouchi-and-masato-shinohara/)

823.

"13 Lakes," is a 2¼-hour film that consists of nothing more than 13 ten-minute shots of lakes. In 2014, it became only the sixth film ever, along with "Raging Bull," "Do the Right Thing," "Goodfellas," "Toy Story" and "Fargo," to be inducted into the National Film Registry in its first year of eligibility.

Reference: (https://en.wikipedia.org/wiki/13_Lakes)

824.

Constance Shulman was picked to be the voice of Patti Mayonnaise on the cartoon "Doug" after the show's creators discovered her on an actual Kraft Mayonnaise commercial.

Reference: (https://www.youtube.com/watch?v=hyrZidwbGzQ)

825.

Wanda Rutkiewicz, a Polish national, was the first woman to climb K2, the second highest peak in the world, in 1986. She was also the first European woman to climb Mount Everest, the highest peak in the world.

Reference: (https://en.wikipedia.org/wiki/Wanda_Rutkiewicz)

826.

A woman was killed by a beach umbrella that was blown by a gust of wind.

Reference:(https://cooperhurley.com/blog/lottie-michelle-belk-is-killed-by-umbrella-in-virginia-beach/)

827.

The maximum possible score in a game of "Jeopardy!" is $566,400 if everything happens in a very specific way.

Reference: (http://datagenetics.com/blog/september12012/index.html)

828.

The origin of the fortune cookie was disputed between a Japanese tea garden in South Francisco and a noodle maker in Los Angeles. When the case reached the South Francisco Court of Historical Review, a fortune cookie was brought as evidence. It read: "S.F. Judge who rules for L.A. Not Very Smart Cookie". The court decided on San Francisco.

Reference: (https://en.wikipedia.org/wiki/Fortune_cookie)

829.

A 20th century biologist discovered so many species of moths that he simply named them E. bobana, E. cocana, E. dodana, E. fofana, E. hohana, E. kokana, E. lolana and E. momana.

Reference:(https://www.smithsonianmag.com/science-nature/the-worlds-strangest-scientific-names-14139154/)

830.

The batman, about 7.7 kilograms, is a unit of mass that was used in certain regions of the Ottoman Empire.

Reference: (https://www.revolvy.com/page/Ottoman-units-of-measurement?cr=1)

831.

There are 2 definitions of when a "Century" starts and ends. Strictly speaking, the "20th Century" didn't end until December 31, 2000.

Reference: (https://en.wikipedia.org/wiki/Century)

832.

A British man named Robert Fidler asked for permission to build a mini castle on his farm. Permission was not granted, so he built it secretly and hid it behind haystacks for 4 years, believing that if nobody complained for 4 years he could keep it.

Reference: (https://en.wikipedia.org/wiki/Honeycrock_Farm)

833.

Julia Louis-Dreyfus' family owns and runs one of the richest companies on earth, the Louis Dreyfus Company. They have over $120 billion in gross sales per year and have companies in over 100 countries. Her father was a billionaire.

Reference:(https://en.wikipedia.org/wiki/Louis_Dreyfus_Company)

834.

As a result of the Stock Market Crash of 1929, the world stopped the majority of imports of coffee from Brazil, so in 1932 they used coffee beans as fuel for locomotives.

Reference: (https://makezine.com/2007/01/17/using-coffee-as-fuel-in-b/)

835.

On a global scale, the population "explosion" of the previous century is over.

Reference:(https://climateandcapitalism.com/2010/08/31/the-greening-of-hate-an-environmentalists-essay/)

836.

The popular MMO "EVE Online" hired an economist to oversee the in-game money. Besides writing internal reports, he occasionally intervenes to prevent inflation and unintended market consequences. EVE has about 500,000 users who partake in the game's hyper-libertarian online economy.

Reference:(https://www.fastcompany.com/3024392/meet-the-alan-greenspan-of-virtual-currency-in-eve-online)

837.

A coffin is shaped specifically for a human body, while a casket is simply a box for important things.

Reference: (https://www.differencebetween.com/difference-between-coffin-and-vs-casket/)

838.

Since 2000, 52% of Fortune 500 companies are gone as a result of digital disruption.

Reference:(https://hbr.org/sponsored/2017/07/digital-transformation-is-racing-ahead-and-no-industry-is-immune-2)

839.

In developmental psychology, there are more studies of non-humans primates than of Africans, Asians or Latin Americans.

Reference:(https://www.uni-muenster.de/imperia/md/content/psyifp/aekaertner/nielsen__m.__haun__d.__k__rtner__j.____le gare__c.__2017_._the_persistent_sampling_bias_in_developmental_psychology.pdf)

840.

Without Alaska, the United States has a smaller area than Brazil.

Reference: (https://en.wikipedia.org/wiki/Contiguous_United_States)

841.

A Canadian's mistake at the end of World War II almost botched Japan's surrender document.

Reference:(https://www.theglobeandmail.com/news/world/how-a-canadians-mistake-70-years-ago-almost-botched-japans-surrender-document/article26201436/)

842.

Facial hair doesn't "stop growing", but rather each follicle has a limited lifespan. People who can grow longer beards have follicles that survive for longer before falling out.

Reference: (https://wisebeards.com/beards/beard-stop-growing/)

843.

The Mona Lisa Effect is the impression that the eyes of the person in an image follow the viewer as they move in front of the picture. However, two researchers from the Cluster found that the Mona Lisa does not accurately represent the so-called Mona Lisa Effect.

Reference: (https://www.scitecheuropa.eu/mona-lisa-effect/92049/)

844.

The Pen-tailed treeshrew, a small mammal from Thailand, consumes the equivalent of 10 to 12 glasses of wine a night in the form of fermented nectar from the bertam palm. This nectar has an alcohol content of up to 3.8%.

Reference: (https://en.wikipedia.org/wiki/Pen-tailed_treeshrew)

845.

A bottle of Coca-Cola cost one nickel between 1886 and 1959. The price remained fixed with very little fluctuation. In 1953, Coca-Cola approached the U.S. Treasury to request minting a 7.5 cent coin.

Reference: (https://en.wikipedia.org/wiki/Fixed_price_of_Coca-Cola_from_1886_to_1959)

846.

The Annapurna peaks are among the world's most dangerous to climb, having been 191 summit ascents, and 61 climbing fatalities on the mountain. Killing 1 person for every 4 who make it to the top.

Reference: (https://en.wikipedia.org/wiki/Annapurna_Massif)

847.

During World War II, British Intelligence dressed up a dead tramp as a Royal Marine Officer. They placed personal items on the tramp, including correspondence between two generals that the Allies planned to invade Greece and Sardinia. This deception drew German forces away from the true target, Sicily.

Reference: (https://en.wikipedia.org/wiki/Operation_Mincemeat)

848.

Christmas was banned by Parliament in 1644 and abolished in 1647. The army actively stopped people from celebrating Christmas. Oliver Cromwell and the Puritans thought Christmas festivities were sinful, wasteful, and had no biblical justification.

Reference: (https://www.nam.ac.uk/explore/war-christmas)

849.

For a decade in the 1920s, the Eiffel tower was the world's largest billboard. As dusk fell hundreds of lights were turned on to illuminate the name of the car manufacturer Citroën.

Reference:(https://www.autocar.co.uk/car-news/industry/throwback-thursday-citro%C3%ABn-lights-eiffel-tower-4-july-1925)

850.

Julie d'Aubigny was a 17th-century traveling swordswoman. Among her other exploits, when her female lover was sent to a convent, she also entered the convent, stole the body of a dead nun, placed it in her lover's bed, escaped with her lover and burnt the convent down.

Reference: (http://www.badassoftheweek.com/lamaupin.html)

851.

The legend of Unsinkable Sam is about a ship's cat in World War II that might have survived 3 sinkings of battleships.

Reference: (https://en.wikipedia.org/wiki/Unsinkable_Sam)

852.

There are people who believe that at least 300 years of the Middle Ages have been invented by a few rulers, so they could live in the year 1,000.

Reference: (https://en.wikipedia.org/wiki/Phantom_time_hypothesis)

853.

The sign for German in some sign languages symbolizes a spiked helmet due to the historical headgear worn by the German military and police.

Reference: (http://www.lifeprint.com/asl101/pages-signs/g/germany.htm)

854.

Betamax wasn't discontinued until 2016.

Reference: (https://en.wikipedia.org/wiki/Betamax)

855.

Ian Benardo, an American Idol contestant who, incensed at Simon Cowell calling his act "rubbish", demanded to see his work visa.

Reference: (https://nypost.com/2007/01/25/n-y-idol-booted-for-slimin-simon/)

856.

Ferdinand Porsche stole several design elements of the Volkswagen Beetle from an Austrian engineer named Hans Ledwinka of Tatra, a Czech car company. Tatra took legal action, but Hitler invaded Austria, seized its factory, and banned the car. The case was settled by Volkswagen after the war.

Reference: (http://www.bbc.com/culture/story/20130830-the-nazi-car-we-came-to-love)

857.

Italy and Ethiopia went to war because of a misunderstanding caused by a verb.

Reference: (https://en.wikipedia.org/wiki/Treaty_of_Wuchale)

858.

In 1924, Harold Israel was a vagrant accused of the murder of a priest. All the evidence seemed to fit him, but in court, the prosecutor Homer Cummings logically tore the case against him to shreds and freed him. Years later, Homer contacted him to share money from a film deal based on the case.

Reference:(https://www.smithsonianmag.com/history/charming-story-homer-cummings-harold-israel-180961429/)

859.

In 1982, 7 people in Chicago died after taking Tylenol laced with potassium cyanide. No suspect was ever charged or convicted.

Reference: (https://en.wikipedia.org/wiki/Chicago_Tylenol_murders)

860.

Seafarers have a mandatory rest of only 77 hours a week. In a 24 hour period, 10 hours of rest with one period of rest being at least 6 hours and the other 4 divided. That's a potential 91 hours of labor per week.

Reference:(https://www.marineinsight.com/maritime-law/the-ultimate-guide-to-work-hours-rest-hours-on-ships-including-stcw-2010/)

861.

Beaches south of Perth get smaller waves due to the Rottnest Island Effect.

Reference: (https://www.gosurfperth.com/blog/2016/9/2/where-to-surf-in-perth-1)

862.

In the Dyatlov Pass Incident, in 1959, 9 experienced hikers mysteriously died in the freezing Ural Mountains after fleeing their tent. Most were in their underwear, 1 had a fractured skull, another had tongue and eyes missing. Circumstances remain a mystery to this day.

Reference: (https://www.cnn.com/2019/02/04/europe/dyatlov-pass-incident-scli-intl/index.html)

863.

Scientific American magazine welcomes essays from writers and scholars at all levels, from grad students and postdocs to senior researchers. However, articles must present ideas that have already been published and peer-reviewed as they do not publish new theories or results of original research.

Reference: (https://www.scientificamerican.com/page/submission-instructions/)

864.

The left testicle usually hangs a little lower than the one on the right, and it's no accident. This allows the temperature of one testis to change without that energy being sent to the other. The body can increase or decrease the temperature of one testis without affecting the temperature of the other.

Reference: (https://www.health.com/sexual-health/testicle-facts)

865.

"Sunbursts" in photos have twice many sun rays as aperture blades.

Reference:(https://petapixel.com/2018/05/19/the-physics-behind-sunbursts-and-how-it-can-help-you-focus-your-photos/)

866.

The song "Eternity" from the 2006 video game, "Blue Dragon," was performed by Ian Gillan of Deep Purple fame, who is one of the major musical influences for composer Nobuo Uematsu.

Reference:(https://www.gameinformer.com/b/features/archive/2014/07/10/the-goofiest-video-game-lyrics.aspx)

867.

Willie Sutton, a bank robber in the early 1900's, stole an estimated $2 million over a 40 year career. He never robbed a bank with a loaded gun because he didn't want anyone to get hurt, and allegedly never robbed a bank when a woman screamed or a baby cried. He escaped prison 3 times.

Reference: (https://en.wikipedia.org/wiki/Willie_Sutton)

868.

In the 1690s, women had pockets tied around their waist, between the under-petticoat and petticoat. Openings in the side seams allowed them to put their hands through and reach their pockets.

Reference: (http://www.vam.ac.uk/content/articles/a/history-of-pockets/)

869.

Saddam Hussein wrote a romance novel called "Zabibah and the King"; it has sold over a million copies.

Reference: (https://en.wikipedia.org/wiki/Zabibah_and_the_King)

870.

The Illusion of Explanatory Depth, similar to the Dunning-Kruger effect, is the powerful but inaccurate feeling of knowing something in greater detail than you really do.

Reference: (https://www.edge.org/response-detail/27117)

871.

People in the final stages of hypothermia engage in "paradoxical undressing" because, as they lose rationality and their nerves are damaged, they feel incredibly, irrationally hot. They strip off their clothes to cool themselves down as they are freezing to death and then start burrowing.

Reference:(https://io9.gizmodo.com/why-freezing-to-death-makes-you-want-to-get-naked-1688151366/amp)

872.

In 1948, Kurt Gödel produced a solution of Einstein's gravitational field equations that described a rotating universe and showed that going back in time was not forbidden by the theory of relativity. In this universe, an astronaut could travel through space so as to reach his own past.

Reference: (https://www.nikhef.nl/pub/services/biblio/bib_KR/sciam14327036.pdf)

873.

The longest-running experiment is the Pitch Drop Experiment. A funnel holding a sample of tar pitch sealed in a glass jar shows how some substances that appear solid are actually liquid. It takes 10 years for a single drop to form. The best known version of the experiment was started in 1927.

Reference: (https://en.wikipedia.org/wiki/Pitch_drop_experiment)

874.

Only 12.6% of China's total land area is suitable for growing crops.

Reference: (https://en.wikipedia.org/wiki/Agriculture_in_China)

875.

According to the crew cabin recorder in the Challenger space shuttle during the disaster, the last words of the crewmembers was spoken by pilot Michael Smith: "Uh-oh." It is unknown what he was pointing out.

Reference: (https://en.wikipedia.org/wiki/Space_Shuttle_Challenger_disaster#Vehicle_breakup)

876.

Men's motives for buying sex are hotly contested among researchers. There are no social characteristics that basically distinguish "johns" from other men nor are these men defined by obvious personality problems.

Reference: (http://library.allanschore.com/docs/Your_Sexual_Brain.pdf)

877.

The ingredients of desire may differ for men and women, but researchers have revealed some surprising similarities. For example, visual stimuli spur sexual stirrings in women, as they do in men.

Reference:(http://paulocoelhoblog.com/2008/05/16/the-orgasmic-mind-the-neurological-roots-of-sexual-pleasure/)

878.

The U.S. in the 1980s had a "Satanic Panic" whereby hundreds of daycare centres were falsely accessed on satanic rituals on children.

Reference:(https://www.vox.com/2016/10/30/13413864/satanic-panic-ritual-abuse-history-explained)

879.

Bottlenose dolphin in Hawaii asked divers for help.

Reference: (https://www.youtube.com/watch?v=2gvgkHSyKFE&feature=youtu.be)

880.

Despite its incredible length, the neck of a giraffe only contains 7 vertebrae; the same number humans have.

Reference: (https://animals.howstuffworks.com/mammals/giraffe-neck.htm)

881.

Many courses in German Universities are actually offered in English, and international students don't even have to meet the German language requirements to apply. In Germany, undergraduate students don't pay any tuition fees in all the public universities since October, 2014.

Reference:(https://www.studyandgoabroad.com/hot-news/germany-offering-free-tuition-canadian-students/)

882.

A university called 42 is free, doesn't care about SAT scores and wants to educate 10,000 students within the next 5 years. When the French President visited the campus in Paris there were students sleeping on the floor in the hallway.

Reference:(https://techcrunch.com/2016/05/17/coding-school-42-plans-to-educate-10000-students-in-silicon-valley-for-free/)

883.

The actor that played Juan in the movie "The Big Green" was a successful college soccer player and is now Assistant Head Coach for the Furman University Men's Soccer Team.

Reference:(https://www.furmanpaladins.com/sports/m-soccer/coaches/Esquivel_Anthony?view=bio)

884.

The NYPD has a beekeeper unit.

Reference:(https://www.newyorker.com/magazine/2018/09/17/when-bees-go-rogue-call-the-nypd)

885.

The Washington Times newspaper was formed by Sun Myung Moon, the leader of the Unification movement.

Reference: (https://en.wikipedia.org/wiki/The_Washington_Times)

886.

The last film Sean Connery was ever in was an animated flop called "Sir Billi," which was about a skateboarding veterinarian who fights the police to help a fugitive beaver.

Reference: (https://en.wikipedia.org/wiki/Sir_Billi

887.

Russia and China are currently the only two crewed spacefaring nations.

Reference: (https://en.wikipedia.org/wiki/Spacefaring#Crewed_spacefaring_nations)

888.

Duck embryos are a delicacy in the Philippines.

Reference: (https://en.wikipedia.org/wiki/Balut_(food))

889.

Jeff Bezos and George Strait are cousins through Bezos's grandmother.

Reference:(https://www.statesman.com/news/20180405/heres-your-friendly-reminder-that-jeff-bezos-is-george-straits-cousin)

890.

A group of owls is called a "wisdom" or a "parliament".

Reference: (https://www.owlpages.com/owls/articles.php?a=96)

891.

Families were forced to leave pets behind after the Chernobyl Meltdown, pets who were then hunted and killed by squads of Soviet soldiers.

Reference: (https://cleanfutures.org/projects/dogs-of-chernobyl/)

892.

In 2015, Tyler The Creator was banned from entering the U.K. for 3 to 5 years because of lyrics from his albums "Bastard" and "Goblin".

Reference:(https://www.ballerstatus.com/2015/08/26/tyler-the-creator-banned-from-u-k-forced-to-cancel-shows/)

893.

From the 40% of newborns born with a "stork bite" birthmark, 50% of those carry the mark into adulthood.

Reference: (https://www.aafp.org/afp/1998/0215/p765.html)

894.

There are 70,000 Mennonites living in Bolivia. They originated in Europe then moved to North America then to Bolivia. Their communities are completely insular.

Reference:(https://www.nationalgeographic.com/photography/proof/2018/february/mennonites-bolivia-busque/)

895.

Sleep Texting occurs when the brain and body are in a state that's not fully awake, but not entirely asleep either and someone responds to the sound their smartphone makes when they receive a message.

Reference: (https://www.sleepadvisor.org/sleep-texting/)

896.

On August 26, 1990, Stevie Ray Vaughan described a disturbing dream to his band mates in which he witnessed his own funeral. The next day, he tragically died in a helicopter crash.

Reference: (https://www.guitarworld.com/artists/august-1990-how-stevie-ray-vaughan-died)

897.

In California, survivors of the Pearl Harbor Attack can get a special licence plate to commemorate the event.

Reference: (https://www.dmv.ca.gov/portal/dmv/detail/pubs/reg_hdbk/ch21/ch21_36)

898.

The Chernobyl Meltdown caused cancer increases as far away as Sweden.

Reference: (https://expertsvar.se/en/pressmeddelanden/chernobyl-disaster-caused-cancer-cases-in-sweden/)

899.

Bacteria in your gut help mold your brain as an infant, altering brain development and neuroplasticity. The bacteria also influence brain activity and behavior in the human brain as an adult.

Reference: (https://www.karger.com/Article/FullText/366281)

900.

The green Haribo gummy bear is strawberry flavored.

Reference:(https://www.thedailymeal.com/eat/5-things-you-didnt-know-about-haribo-gummy-bears)

901.

Plywood glue is often made with cow blood.

Reference:(https://adhesives.specialchem.com/formulation/blood-glue-for-plywood-and-packaging)

902.

The singer of the punk classic "Hit Me With Your Rhythm Stick" contracted polio at age 7. The disease left him crippled and barely 5 feet tall.

Reference: (https://www.theguardian.com/culture/2009/nov/29/ian-dury-popandrock)

903.

In 2018, Ukraine spent 5% to 7% of its annual government budget on recovery and cleanup efforts related to the Chernobyl Disaster.

Reference: (https://en.wikipedia.org/wiki/Chernobyl_disaster#Social_economic_effect)

904.

In 26 states, it is legal for insurance companies to deny claims if you are injured as a result of being drunk.

Reference: (https://www.insurance.com/health-insurance/coverage/alcohol-claim-denial.html)

905.

Postage stamps weren't always prepaid. Some of the first post offices in the 1840s made recipients pay for their mail, and only if they came to pick it up. This led to postage going unpaid, a decrease in revenue, and the creation of federal postage stamps.

Reference: (https://postalmuseum.si.edu/research/finding-guides/1847-postage-stamp-correspondence.html)

906.

Barney Martin, who played Morty Seinfeld, was an NYPD Detective, and continued to be one well into his acting career.

Reference: (https://en.wikipedia.org/wiki/Barney_Martin)

907.

Titanic became, on March 1, 1998, the first movie to gross over $1 billion worldwide.

Reference: (https://en.wikipedia.org/wiki/List_of_fastest-grossing_films)

908.

Starting with season six, Roseanne Barr had all of the writers of "Roseanne" wear shirts with numbers on them. She would refer to them only by their number.

Reference: (https://variety.com/1993/tv/news/roseanne-to-writers-take-a-number-109869/)

909.

In the 1970s, the risk of acquiring Hepatitis C from a blood transfusion was 1 in 10. Since 1992, it has decreased to 1 in two million thanks to widespread screening of blood.

Reference: (https://en.wikipedia.org/wiki/Hepatitis#Infectious)

910.

The orphaned children of executed spies Julius and Ethel Rosenberg were adopted by the man who wrote the anti-lynching song "Strange Fruit".

Reference: (https://en.wikipedia.org/wiki/Abel_Meeropol)

911.

When the remains from an overcrowded Paris cemetery were moved to the catacombs, the "corpse wax" from partially decomposed bodies was used to make soap.

Reference: (https://en.wikipedia.org/wiki/Holy_Innocents%27_Cemetery)

912.

A force called The Batman Battalion fought in the ongoing war in Donbass, Ukraine.

Reference: (https://en.wikipedia.org/wiki/Separatist_forces_of_the_war_in_Donbass#Structure)

913.

Sean Connery younger brother Neil, starred in "O.K. Connery", a James Bond-inspired film. The film was retitled "Operation Kid Brother" in the United States and is also known as "Operation Double 007."

Reference: (https://en.wikipedia.org/wiki/Neil_Connery)

914.

The Taj Mahal was built at a cost estimated at the time to be around 32 million rupees, which would be approximately 52.8 billion rupees today.

Reference: (https://en.wikipedia.org/wiki/Taj_Mahal)

915.

The feral child Marcos Rodríguez Pantoja was sold by his family to work as a slave and was raised by wolves for 12 years. When found by the civil guard at the age of 19, the father recognized his son, but faced no charges at all for selling him and only reproached Pantoja for having lost his jacket.

Reference: (https://en.wikipedia.org/wiki/Marcos_Rodr%C3%ADguez_Pantoja)

916.

Maggie Q has a scripted phrase running alongside her left torso which reads: "umuntu ngumuntu ngabantu".

Reference: (https://stealherstyle.net/maggie-q/?post_type=tattoos)

917.

Generation Starships, interstellar travel ships that take centuries to reach their destination, were first described in concept in 1929 by J.D. Bernal.

Reference: (https://en.wikipedia.org/wiki/Generation_ship)

918.

Alcatraz's reputation as a tough as nails prison was a Hollywood myth. Many inmates requested transfer there on account of its good food and one man per cell policy.

Reference: (https://www.history.com/news/10-things-you-may-not-know-about-alcatraz)

919.

Frank Sinatra was originally the first choice as John McClane in the film "Die Hard." He was 73 when he turned down the role that eventually went to Bruce Willis.

Reference:(https://www.independent.co.uk/arts-entertainment/films/features/die-hard-30th-anniversary-john-mctiernan-action-movie-bruce-willis-a8441581.html)

920.

Mike Myers stole the characterization of Dr. Evil from Dana Carvey's original impersonation of legendary Saturday Night Live producer, Lorne Michaels. This didn't sit well with Carvey who admits to having had to address it in therapy as for closure.

Reference: (https://www.youtube.com/watch?v=MutuEJh0snE&feature=youtu.be)

921.

The longest professional baseball game was a 1981 minor league game between the Pawtucket Red Sox and the Rochester Red Wings. It lasted 33 innings. The first 32 were played April 18 to 19, and the final inning was played June 23. Pawtucket won 3 to 2.

Reference: (https://en.wikipedia.org/wiki/Longest_professional_baseball_game)

922.

When the world's largest hailstone was found in South Dakota, the man who found the stone originally intended to make cocktails using the ice before deciding to hand over the stone to the National Weather Service.

Reference:(https://www.wunderground.com/blog/weatherhistorian/worlds-largest-hailstones.html)

923.

It can snow when the temperature outside is above freezing if the upper atmosphere is at or below freezing, and an evaporative cooling effect surrounding the snowflakes protects them from melting as they fall through warmer air to the ground.

Reference: (https://nsidc.org/cryosphere/snow/science/formation.html)

924.

Someone tried to steal George Washington's skull from the Washington family crypt in 1830, but accidentally stole the skull of one of Washington's nephew's in-laws.

Reference: (https://en.wikipedia.org/wiki/Attempted_theft_of_George_Washington%27s_skull)

925.

The 1992 Emmys removed the "Outstanding Guest Actor/Actress" categories from the ceremony, leading to many actors getting major acting nominations for guest appearances, most notably Christopher Lloyd winning "Outstanding Lead Actor in a Drama" for a single appearance on "Road to Avonlea."

Reference: (https://emmys.com/awards/nominees-winners/1992)

926.

There is an "erotic" section of the Bible that described intimacy, desire, and sexual love.

Reference: (https://en.wikipedia.org/wiki/Song_of_Songs)

927.

Robert E. Lee opposed building public memorials to the Confederacy. Shortly after his death, admirers made him the centerpiece of the "Lost Cause of the Confederacy" movement.

Reference:(https://www.nytimes.com/2017/08/22/us/lee-family-confederate-monuments-legacy.html)

928.

King Henry VIII's first wife, Catherine of Aragon, was the First Female Ambassador in European History, as ambassador of Aragon to England.

Reference: (https://en.wikipedia.org/wiki/Catherine_of_Aragon)

929.

Cattle and dog dewormer Ivermectin is also effective at treating some cancers.

Reference:(https://www.ncbi.nlm.nih.gov/pmc/articles/PMC5835698/e)

930.

Sean Connery once beat up four men single-handedly for giving some girls a hard time in a club, while Michael Caine held his coat.

Reference:(https://www.dailystar.co.uk/news/latest-news/158913/Michael-Caine-s-hooked-on-007)

931.

In 1120, the captain of the White Ship was encouraged by on-board revelers to try and overtake another vessel on which King Henry I was a passenger. In the dark, the ship hit a submerged rock and capsized, leading to the death of Henry's only heir, which led to a 20 year civil war.

Reference: (https://en.wikipedia.org/wiki/White_Ship)

932.

Qatar Airlines allows falcons, up to 6, to fly in-cabin, but no other pets are allowed.

Reference: (https://www.bringfido.com/travel/airline_policies/qatar_airways/)

933.

The Cooper Vane is an aerodynamic wedge on the rear of an airplane that prevents the rear stairs from lowering. It is named after the legendary D.B. Cooper who hijacked a plane, demanded a $1,240,000, adjusted, ransom, and escaped from the flying plane via a parachute and the rear stairs.

Reference: (https://en.wikipedia.org/wiki/Cooper_vane)

934.

Maria Grazia "Lella" Lombardi is the only woman ever to score points in a Formula 1 auto race, and that was by finishing sixth in a shortened race.

Reference:(https://jalopnik.com/lella-lombardi-is-the-only-woman-to-ever-score-points-i-1831436326)

935.

In 1982, the comic strip "The Far Side" jokingly referred to the set of spikes on a Stegosaurus's tail as a "thagomizer". A paleontologist who read the comic realized that there wasn't any official name for the spikes and began using the new word; Thagomizer is now the generally accepted term.

Reference: (https://en.wikipedia.org/wiki/Thagomizer)

936.

Pencils are yellow due to American manufacturers trying to communicate a feeling of "luxury" with China, due to yellow being associated with regality and royalty in China.

Reference: (https://www.artsy.net/article/artsy-editorial-little-known-reason-pencils-yellow/amp)

937.

Robert Frost was the first poet to read at a presidential inauguration when John F. Kennedy asked him to recite a poem at his in 1961. Frost wrote a new poem for the occasion, but was incapable of reading it because of how bright it was outside. So, he recited "The Gift Outright" from memory instead.

Reference: (https://poets.org/text/poetry-and-power-robert-frosts-inaugural-reading)

938.

The director of "Mrs. Doubtfire" also directed "Home Alone," the first two "Harry Potter Films," "Rent," "Percy Jackson" and "Pixels."

Reference: (https://en.wikipedia.org/wiki/Mrs._Doubtfire)

939.

Christopher Mintz-Plasse was only 17 when he filmed "Superbad", so his mother was required to be on set for his sex scene.

Reference: (https://en.wikipedia.org/wiki/Superbad_(film)#Principal_photography)

940.

The English monarchy protected peasant and public lands from the privatizing force of "Enclosure," where such lands were consolidated into larger farms. After the monarchy lost power, Enclosure accelerated unabated until the peasant community was destroyed and little public land was left.

Reference: (https://en.wikipedia.org/wiki/Enclosure#Parliamentary_enclosure_and_open_fields)

941.

After being hired as a mercenary to overthrow the president of Equatorial Guinea, and failing, Simon Mann befriended the president while in jail and was hired as a presidential adviser upon release.

Reference:(https://www.independent.co.uk/news/world/africa/mann-back-in-equatorial-guinea-ndash-to-work-for-leader-he-tried-to-oust-2115646.html)

942.

Wilhelm Karl von Urach was a German Duke who, at different times, was heir to the throne of Monaco, King-Elect of Lithuania, and candidate for the thrones of Albania, Alsace-Lorraine, and Württemberg.

Reference: (https://en.wikipedia.org/wiki/Wilhelm_Karl,_Duke_of_Urach)

943.

When doctors can't establish an IV line, they can use a technique which is nearly equal in effectiveness: intraosseous infusion. They hammer a needle directly through a bone into the marrow to deliver fluids.

Reference: (https://en.wikipedia.org/wiki/Intraosseous_infusion)

944.

In Europe, you can get hot French fries in less than 2 minutes from a French fry vending machine.

Reference:(https://www.today.com/food/best-invention-ever-french-fry-vending-machine-I545634)

945.

The catacombs of Paris are only a small part of the mines, or quarries, of Paris, an extensive gypsum deposit under the city from which we get "plaster of Paris".

Reference: (https://en.wikipedia.org/wiki/Mines_of_Paris)

946.

The tanuki, also known as "Japanese Raccoon Dog", is neither a raccoon or a dog.

Reference: (https://en.wikipedia.org/wiki/Japanese_raccoon_dog)

947.

Besides cats and dogs, John F. Kennedy also had a pair of Syrian hamsters, Debbie and Billie. After Debbie gave birth to a litter of pups, one of the pups drowned in a bathtub and Billie ate the rest. Debbie then ate Billie, and died of indigestion.

Reference: (http://www.presidentialpetmuseum.com/pets/jfk-hamsters-debbie-billie/)

948.

"Breakfast is the most important meal of the day" was an ad slogan invented in the 19th century by Seventh Day Adventists James Caleb Jackson and John Harvey Kellogg to sell their newly invented breakfast cereal.

Reference:(https://www.daytwo.com/blog/nutrition-myths-facts-series-part-1-breakfast-important-meal-day/)

949.

In the film "Look Who's Talking," Albert, the womanizing executive and biological father of Mikey, is a representation of Harold Ramis who had an affair and child with the film's writer and director, Amy Heckerling.

Reference:(https://www.vulture.com/2018/06/the-story-of-harold-ramis-and-amy-heckerlings-daughter.html)

950.

Only two assassination attempts on U.S. Presidents have been made by women. Both happened within 3 weeks of each other in California against Gerald Ford. They were apparently unrelated.

Reference:(https://en.wikipedia.org/wiki/List_of_United_States_presidential_assassination_attempts_and_plots#Gerald_Ford)

951.

Racing driver Jim Clark won his second F1 World Championship, the Indy 500, the Tasman Cup, the French F2 Championship and numerous saloon and sports car races, all in one year.

Reference:(https://peterwindsor.com/2015/01/28/jim-clarks-epic-1965-season/)

952.

There isn't really a market for rhino horn as an aphrodisiac and media spreading that myth actually curtails conservation efforts because it perpetuates the myth that wasn't even there in the first place, causing more demand.

Reference:(https://www.scientificamerican.com/article/the-hard-truth-about-the-rhino-horn-aphrodisiac-market/?redirect=1)

953.

The USS Cavalla was a World War II submarine that, on its first war patrol in 1944, sank the IJN carrier Shōkaku that was one of 6 involved in the Pearl Harbor attack and whose aircraft sank the USS Lexington at Coral Sea and crippled the USS Hornet at Santa Cruz.

Reference: (https://en.wikipedia.org/wiki/USS_Cavalla_%28SS-244%29)

954.

Albert Stevens, in 1945, was misdiagnosed as having terminal cancer and injected with plutonium isotopes as part of a radiation experiment. He survived exposure to the highest known radiation dose in any human and lived for another 20 years.

Reference: (https://en.wikipedia.org/wiki/Albert_Stevens)

955.

During San Francisco's Gold Rush, period criminal immigrants from Australia terrorized the city so badly that they set fire to the city 6 times just to distract people from pillaging and murdering until one of the largest Vigilante groups in U.S. history organized to get rid of them.

Reference: (https://en.wikipedia.org/wiki/Barbary_Coast,_San_Francisco#cite_ref-auto2_9-0)

956.

The grandfather of Peter Serafinowicz, the voice of Darth Maul, was the first man in the U.K. to have been tried under the War Crimes Act.

Reference: (https://en.wikipedia.org/wiki/Peter_Serafinowicz#Personal_life)

957.

Genetic variations may make some people's brain more open to thoughts, sensations and behaviors that don't make it past the average person's mental filters. These same variations may also explain why many highly creative people seem eccentric at times, or even suffer from mental illness.

Reference: (https://www.scientificamerican.com/article/inspired-the-science-of-creativity1/)

958.

The human body is only made up of 43% "human" cells. The other 57% is comprised of bacteria, fungi and single-celled eukaryote. Bacteria far outnumber fungi and other microbes, and most of these microbes are found in the gut, thus almost all of the 57 percent are intestinal bacteria.

Reference:(https://melmagazine.com/en-us/story/only-43-of-our-bodies-are-made-up-of-human-cells-so-whats-the-other-57)

959.

Big Dick Data is a formal academic term coined to denote big data projects that have masculinist, totalizing fantasies of world domination through data capture and analysis. Big Dick Data projects ignore context, fetishize size, and overstate, inflate their technical and scientific capabilities.

Reference: (https://bookbook.pubpub.org/pub/6ui5n4vo)

960.

In general, Balinese people name their children depending on the order they are born, and the names are the same for both males and females. The firstborn child is named Wayan, Putu or

Gede, the second is named Made or Kadek, the third child goes by Nyoman or Komang, and the fourth is named Ketu.

Reference: (https://www.ultimatebali.com/magazine/balinese-names-explained/)

961.

Tom Morello's great uncle was Jomo Kenyatta, the first elected president of Kenya.

Reference: (https://en.wikipedia.org/wiki/Kenyatta_family)

962.

The French Republican calendar sought to modernize the measure of time with 10 days per week, 10 hours per day, 100 minutes per hour, and 100 seconds per minute.

Reference: (https://en.wikipedia.org/wiki/French_Republican_calendar)

963.

Soviet leader Nikita Khrushchev gifted U.S. President John F. Kennedy a dog called Pushinka during the Cold War. She later on had puppies; which Kennedy referred to as "the pupniks".

Reference: (https://www.bbc.com/news/magazine-24837199)

964.

Fiat Chrysler Automobiles' head office is located in Amsterdam, Netherlands, and their financial office is in London, U.K., where the company pays its tax.

Reference: (https://en.wikipedia.org/wiki/Fiat_Chrysler_Automobiles)

965.

Albanian Sworn Virgins are women who would take a vow of celibacy and live as men in Albania's patriarchal mountain societies.

Reference: (https://en.wikipedia.org/wiki/Albanian_sworn_virgins)

966.

All dog breeds living with people indigenous to the Americas are extinct.

Reference: (https://en.wikipedia.org/wiki/Native_American_dogs)

967.

Eskimos don't actually have 100 words for "snow".

Reference: (https://en.wikipedia.org/wiki/Eskimo_words_for_snow)

968.

The human sense of smell is comparable to that of a dog.

Reference:(https://www.theguardian.com/science/2017/may/11/not-to-be-sniffed-at-human-sense-of-smell-rivals-that-of-dogs-says-study)

969.

The New York Stock Exchange is owned by a company headquartered in Atlanta, called the Intercontinental Exchange.

Reference: (https://en.wikipedia.org/wiki/Intercontinental_Exchange)

970.

Steven Spielberg thought the "E.T." video game for the Atari 2600 would be too complicated, and told the programmer to just make a Pac-Man clone instead.

Reference:(https://www.npr.org/2017/05/31/530235165/total-failure-the-worlds-worst-video-game)

971.

Until the 1960s, men with long hair were not allowed to enter Disneyland because it did not meet the standards of Disney's unwritten code dress.

Reference: (https://www.snopes.com/fact-check/hair-today/)

972.

Rolls-Royce cars have an anti theft mechanism that retracts the "Spirit of Ecstasy" ornament should it be jostled.

Reference: (https://www.youtube.com/watch?v=aj53HuWBfjE)

973.

In 1969, the U.S. side of Niagara Falls was stopped with a "cofferdam", and it is planned to be stopped again in 2019 to repair the bridges.

Reference:(http://mentalfloss.com/article/74595/heres-how-engineers-plan-stop-flow-niagara-falls)

974.

In 2006, the original 100 year old plaque from The Big Apple Jazz Club in Harlem, from which New York City gets its nickname, was rescued from the trash when a Popeyes fast food restaurant tore down the original building.

Reference:(https://www.barrypopik.com/index.php/new_york_city/entry/harlem_big_apple_club_plaque_removed_2006/)

975.

In the "Short Circuit" movies, the main human character, Ben the Indian scientist, changes name between movies, from Ben Jabituya to Ben Jahveri, yet nobody seems to know why.

Reference: (https://nothingbutnostalgia.com/short-circuit-facts/)

976.

In 2017, Indiana natives won the NBA and D-league Dunk Contests, NBA and D-league 3-point contests, and won runner-up in the NBA Skills Challenge.

Reference: (https://en.wikipedia.org/wiki/Hoosier_Hysteria)

977.

Mad Honey occurs when bees source nectar and pollen from toxic plants and the honey produced has intoxicating effects. This is consumed recreationally in some places.

Reference: (https://www.ncbi.nlm.nih.gov/pmc/articles/PMC3404272/)

978.

Although the number of total donors has declined, Americans donated over $410,000,000,000 to charity in 2017.

Reference:(https://theconversation-com.cdn.ampproject.org/v/s/theconversation.com/amp/fewer-americans-are-giving-money-to-charity-but-total-donations-are-at-record-levels-anyway-98291?usqp=mq331AQA&amp_js_v=0.1#referrer=https%3A%2F%2Fwww.google.com&amp_tf=From%20%251%24s&ampshare=https%3A%2F%2Ftheconversation.com%2Ffewer-americans-are-giving-money-to-charity-but-total-donations-are-at-record-levels-anyway-98291)

979.

In 1897, a scientist named Amos Dolbear published an article "The Cricket as a Thermometer" that noted the correlation between the ambient temperature and the rate at which crickets chirp.

Reference: (https://www.almanac.com/content/predict-temperature-cricket-chirps)

980.

Jordan Brown, the 11 year old who was accused of shooting and killing his mother in 2009, was exonerated of the crime by Pennsylvania's Supreme Court in 2018.

Reference: (https://www.innocenceproject.org/jordan-brown-exonerated-of-2009-murder/)

981.

Woodrow Wilson re-segregated Princeton University when he was the school's president.

Reference: (https://slavery.princeton.edu/stories/erased-pasts-and-altered-legacies-princetons-first-african-american-students)

982.

The maker of SoftSoap knew he couldn't patent liquid soap dispensers, so he did the next best thing: he raised $12 million and bought out the U.S.'s entire manufacturing capacity for two years to prevent other soap companies from stealing his idea.

Reference: (https://www.inc.com/francesca-fenzi/three-shrewd-moves-you-cant-ignore.html)

983.

Bob Vila, famous handyman, was actually fired from "This Old House." They paid him very little money and then demanded he drop his sponsorships that actually brought him income when Home Depot complained.

Reference: (https://tedium.co/2018/09/18/bob-vila-this-old-house-departure/)

984.

A hero cat named Masha saved an abandoned baby from freezing in the cold.

Reference: (https://www.independent.co.uk/news/world/russian-cat-called-masha-saves-baby-abandoned-in-the-cold-9983367.html)

985.

The most popular Atari 2600 game, "Yars' Revenge", and the least popular, "E.T. the Extra Terrestrial," were made by the same guy: Howard Scott Warshaw.

Reference: (https://en.wikipedia.org/wiki/Howard_Scott_Warshaw)

986.

Before there were alarm clocks, there were "knockers-up", who were hired to shoot dried peas from a blow gun at people's windows in order to wake them up in the morning.

Reference: (https://en.wikipedia.org/wiki/Knocker-up)

987.

The original version of "Eminence Front" by The Who has a syncopation in the first chorus where Pete Townshend sings one syllable behind compared to Roger Daltrey. This was later corrected in the remastered version of the song.

Reference: (https://en.wikipedia.org/wiki/Eminence_Front)

988.

Benjamin Lay, an early Quaker abolitionist, walked into the 1738 annual meeting of Quakers and during an abolition speech plunged a sword into a bible he had hollowed out and filled with a bladder full of red fruit juice. To horrified onlookers, the Bible appeared to be bleeding.

Reference: (https://en.wikipedia.org/wiki/Benjamin_Lay#Abolitionism)

989.

Pringles had to use supercomputers to engineer their chips with optimal aerodynamic properties so that they wouldn't fly off the conveyor belts when moving at very high speeds.

Reference: (https://www.hpcwire.com/2006/05/05/high_performance_potato_chips/)

990.

There is a putative type of neuron that reacts to the concept of familiar people. It is dubbed "Jennifer Aniston Neuron" as in a subject a specific neuron was seen firing every time a picture or the name of the actress was delivered.

Reference: (https://en.wikipedia.org/wiki/Grandmother_cell)

991.

Nazi Germany claimed an Antarctic Colony named New Swabia.

Reference: (https://en.wikipedia.org/wiki/New_Swabia)

992.

A polar bear used to live at the Tower of London and go swimming in the Thames. It was a gift from King Haakon of Norway in 1252.

Reference:(https://magazine.trueroyalty.tv/2019/02/21/royal-moments-when-a-polar-bear-lived-at-the-tower-of-london/)

993.

A cat in Canada saved it's family from a fire in the house by biting the arm of the mother who was sleeping and gathered her family and they escaped the burning house without any injuries.

Reference:(https://www.cbsnews.com/news/this-heroic-cat-bit-its-sleeping-owner-to-alert-her-to-house-fire/)

994.

The Honus Wagner (1911) baseball card sold for $3.12 million in 2016. There are only about 25 to 200 copies in existence because Wagner told the American Tobacco Company to pull the card from circulation.

Reference: (http://mentalfloss.com/article/78561/most-valuable-baseball-cards-in-the-world)

995.

"Trout tickling" is a technique for catching trout and other fish using only your hands. While the fish is resting, the poacher will carefully rub his finger against the trout's belly, which causes the trout to fall in a trance from which it is easy to grab and throw it on the ground.

Reference: (https://fishing.wonderhowto.com/news/art-trout-tickling-myth-reality-0113722/)

996.

The unique Asian/African folk sound heard in M.I.A.'s "Paper Planes" directly uses the melody of a 1982 post-punk song from an English rock band, The Clash's "Straight to Hell".

Reference:(https://en.wikipedia.org/wiki/Paper_Planes_(M.I.A._song)#Background_and_production)

997.

Edward Colston was a celebrated philanthropist who supported and endowed schools, almshouses, hospitals and churches, and his name is commemorated in landmarks, streets, schools and even a sweet bun: but he was a slave trader.

Reference: (https://en.wikipedia.org/wiki/Edward_Colston)

998.

Werner Heisenberg, the scientific head of the German nuclear program, heard the news that the United States had dropped an atomic bomb on Hiroshima and didn't believe it.

Reference: (https://www.atomicheritage.org/history/german-atomic-bomb-project)

999.

Cintia Dicker's career modeling and acting for Sports Illustrated and other high paying clients has allowed her to support children's charities in Brazil. A natural redhead, she is ranked as one of the "Top Sexiest" models in the industry

Reference: (https://en.wikipedia.org/wiki/Cintia_Dicker)

1000.

Few places are dirtier than the checkstand conveyor belts at your local supermarket. Going round and round, year after year, conveyor belts may look clean, but they are actually a breeding ground for unwanted bacteria.

Reference:(https://www.foodsafetynews.com/2014/08/hidden-contamination-at-checkout-grocery-conveyor-belts/)

www.ingramcontent.com/pod-product-compliance
Lightning Source LLC
Chambersburg PA
CBHW050334290526
45785CB00011B/2841